THE AGE OF

GOD

A Revolution of Ancient Thought

Dr. Connie Williams
Foreword by Apostle Kito J. Johnson

Published by Melchizedek Global Publishing
Roswell, Georgia

www.MelchizedekGlobal.net

Unless otherwise stated Scriptures are taken from the New King James Bible version, (NKJV).

Editors: Chipo Musikavanhu and Hannah Perez
Cover Design: Joel Sousa
Interior Layout: Ravi Ramgati

ISBN-10: 0-9989502-1-1
ISBN-13: 978-0-9989502-1-1

Published in the United States of America

Dedication

I dedicate this book to my other family: Mother Johnson, Kito's biological mother, who so graciously shares her son with me; Poppy, Kito's biological father, who has been a consistent support, always; Manny and Imani, Kito's biological children, who have become as my own grandchildren. And most of all, Kito, who has filled a hole in my heart and brought healing to my life that I never thought I would ever experience again. I love you Apostle Kito. You are the son I never got to have physically, but I am graced to have you as a spiritual son.

Foreword

As clear as if it was yesterday, I can remember sitting in Biology class on the second floor of the main building at Etowah High School when I heard the teacher say these words: "Heredity determines what you *may* become, but environment determines what you *will* become." These words have stuck with me for more years than I care to admit. Twenty five years later, I have had a myriad of experiences in business and in ministry, and this is one truth that remains apparent. Everyone is born into a set of circumstances that we don't have the ability to choose. For some, those circumstances are ideal in that they create a synergy that gives one the ability to soar into great realms; but for too many others, their environment serves as a paradigm of limitation. Your connections determine your outlook on life, and your outlook on life determines how much you can achieve in this life.

I was born into a family of believers and I was in church all the time growing up; but my experiences were not limited. My mom would take me to her Baptist church two Sundays a month, and the other two Sundays my father would take me to his Methodist church. Occasionally I would visit my great grandmother's Church of God in Christ. My friends allowed me to tag along to their Word-based church, while other friends introduced me to great teaching ministries like Joyce Meyer and charismatic leaders like Bishop T D Jakes. If those experiences aren't varied enough, I also attended a private Catholic school in my formative years. I had many church experiences—so much so, that when I pastored I nearly lauded in the fact that my church was different from many because of my experiences. I vowed to be far from traditional in my style. After all, I thought, someone like myself could be anything but religious.

I've served in ministry since I was a young child. It didn't take a rocket scientist to acknowledge that my environment was consumed with church and the things of God. Nor was it a surprise when I accepted a call to preach the gospel or when I began to pastor a local congregation.

In spite of remarkable progress as a pastor, I woke up after twelve years unfulfilled. As I looked inward to discover why, the answer that became apparent was quite surprising. I discovered how religious I really was. This was difficult to embrace because of my varied experiences; I thought I was far from religious. After all, I was an apostolic leader who blazed a trail in my territory, so much so that ministries today are graced to enter and impact with much more ease. We placed value on intercessory prayer and the flow of the prophetic. Our teaching was empowering and our worship was uninhibited. With all of this, I couldn't possibly be religious. Oh, but was I?

I discovered that I was religious when I realized that every decision I had made in my life was born from my prior conditioning. Instead of making decisions that were authentic for me, I made decisions based on what was acceptable for the church. This not only led to a subtle judgment of those that didn't look like the ideal, it also underscored my general lack of personal fulfillment. What's more is that I perceive I'm not alone. There are many individuals, inside and outside of the church, that have never been given permission to entertain an original thought; a thought void of the opinions, judgments and ideals embraced by their environment.

Dr. Connie Williams gave me my life back. The revelation she shares in this book has served in immeasurable ways to remove ancient scales from the eyes of those who desire more. Transcending religious rhetoric and ancient opinion, the words on the pages that follow contain the power necessary to revolutionize your thinking as you are catapulted into this present *age*.

Apostle Kito J. Johnson
Kito J Johnson Enterprises, LLC

A Note from the Author

All my life, I've heard a sound. Even as a little girl, there was this pervading noise in the atmosphere. I didn't know what it was, but I knew it was a *sad* sound. I could never quite tell where it was coming from, but as I grew in the things of God, I began to see it manifest.

People would see drug-addicts or alcoholics, but I just heard a sound. There would be news of murders or robberies. I heard a sound. People would talk about how the number of unwed mothers, abortions, and unwanted pregnancies were skyrocketing. The morals were draining out of society. I didn't see any of that. I heard an indistinguishable sound coming from people, from places, from things. There was an ever-present groan in the world; an audible yearning for something.

I have since discovered what it is that I've heard all my life. It's the cry of hunger in creation. Creation is groaning for one thing only—for the sons of God to come into their right mind, become the Melchizedek Priesthood, and give communion to all of creation. The communion that it longs for is the life of God.

For this is the famine in the land. It is a famine, not of bread (Word) nor of water (Spirit) but of hearing the proceeding Word of the Lord.

This book is about the Church coming into her right mind. It is about an awakening that is currently taking place among the people of God, and the true Priesthood who ministers to all of creation. Throughout the book, the term "sons" is used to refer to these mature ones, and does not denote gender.

Hebrews 5:12-14 tells us:

> For though by this time you ought to be teachers, you need someone to teach you again the first principles of the oracles of God; and you have come to need milk and not solid food. For everyone who partakes only of milk is unskilled in the word of righteousness, for he is a babe. But solid food belongs to those who are of full age, that is, those who by reason of use have their senses exercised to discern both good and evil.

God has given us His Word. He has given us His Spirit. We have everything we need in order to grow and mature in the faith. By this time, we ought to be teachers and not just listeners. We ought to be able to overflow and impart to others, and not constantly rely on receiving from others. Unfortunately, many in the church today are content to live off milk alone.

I perceive that there is a people who are ready for the strong meat. There are those who are ready to go deep into the heart and mind of God.

This book is for those people.

Table of Contents

Introduction

I did not grow up in church. When I gave my life to Christ in my latter twenties, I was completely green, so my pastor gave me a Bible. I assumed that the idea was for me to read it, so I did. I found it fascinating. I read with no preconceived notions and I had no other perspectives to weigh what I discovered against. The Word came alive for me as I began to see and link patterns and principles throughout the Scriptures. To my surprise, when I began to share what I had learned, I realized that some of my discoveries went against the grain of traditional thinking. In fact, to some, my interpretation was characterized as out-of-the-box, or spooky. People think that some of the things I talk about are unnerving and mysterious. Christians and non-Christians alike may be uncomfortable discussing certain topics—but the truth is that the Gospel itself is mysterious! The Gospel itself may open up other realities that people had not previously been aware of! Paul tells us that we are not to rely on the temporal, perceived things of this world, but are to look to the unseen, eternal things (2 Corinthians 4:18). The author of Hebrews tells us that faith is "the substance of things hoped for, the evidence of things not seen" (Hebrews 11:1). As believers, we deal with other, often unseen, realities as a common practice.

I was chatting with an apostle a while back; I had never spent any significant time with him before so I tried to put him at ease by saying, "I don't mean to be spooky."

He replied, "Dr. Connie you can be spooky if you want to. You talk about a ghost all the time—it's a Holy Ghost, but it's still a ghost." I laughed to myself. Yet, I realized that there does exist a people who embrace the truth found in other dimensions—in the heavens and the atmosphere. Sound spooky?

Believers can sound double-minded because we talk about death and dying, yet we are never going to die. The truth is, we might lay this outer-shell down, but we really will never die. Death has been defeated. Still, there is a second death—living carnally is the same as being dead. It's possible for a person to be dead and still breathing! You can attend church and still be dead. The preacher can be dead; you can have a whole zombie church! Isn't that spooky?

These things are not just spooky from the perspective of the non-believer; believers often find each other spooky as well. Anything that makes certain believers feel uncomfortable is dumped into the ambiguous category "new age". If any Biblical teaching goes beyond their experience, they dismiss it as a new age teaching. However, what they fail to realize is that we are pressing towards the same thing. We are supposed to be comfortable flowing between the realms. We are supposed to be able to see in different dimensions. Jesus walked in two different worlds; He had one foot in the world of the law, which he was fulfilling, wrapping, and closing. He had his other foot in the kingdom, which was to come.

For as long as I can remember, even as a little girl, I've noticed things that others didn't seem to notice. I could be in a room alone and know that I wasn't really alone. Have you ever experienced this? Perhaps you see stuff out of the corner of your eye. Or maybe you are hearing things. This is not spooky; this is your reality. You are not going crazy. This is what happens when people start waking up. God wants you to have such an overflow of the anointing that you are comfortable navigating between the realms. Peter had such an overflow of the anointing that it flowed into his shadow and healed people. This is the anointing just waiting to be loosed upon creation! It's not for you to keep for yourself; you can overflow everywhere you go.

The Church is slowly transforming into her right mind. God is awakening us. We need to step into this calling. We need to pay attention to our dreams. We need to allow our senses to be awakened. Now this is not an excuse for foolishness; we must remain wise and discerning. It is essential that we stay in the Scripture while heeding the voice of the Spirit.

In this book, I am going to show you how God has been awakening me. Sometimes my response to the unnerving things God was showing me was, "I don't know if I'm ready for that or not." Do you know what the Holy Ghost told me?—to just sit with it a minute. In these pages, I am not only going to go deep, I am going to go over the cliff! If this stretches your mind, I know how you feel. Just sit with it for a while.

The Scriptures tell us:

> "Eye has not seen, nor ear heard,
> Nor have entered into the heart of man
> The things which God has prepared for those
> who love Him."

> But God has revealed them to us through His Spirit. For the Spirit searches all things, yes, the deep things of God.
> —1 Corinthians 2:9-10

In His graciousness, God has revealed things to us through His Spirit that were not previously known. What was unlawful in Paul's day has become lawful in our day (2 Corinthians 12:2-4). Things that couldn't be heard or spoken in Paul's day can be heard and spoken in this day. There are some things that have been sealed up until now (Revelation 6:1).

The Lord is beginning to loose the seals off the books of our understanding—the book that is us. We are the book of the Lamb's life. We are written epistles read of all men. We are a formula for how God works. We are a book with instructions on how He moves and what he does. We are unsealing even hidden things within ourselves, things that we weren't even aware of.

Our vision will be restored, and it will begin to line up with the Father's vision. We will begin to see things that we thought were accidents in a new light. We will begin to understand that things we attribute to the devil are working according to God's plan, according to our favor. God is revealing mysteries to us. Let's awaken to our true calling and step into the mysteries of God!

Chapter 1
The Great Awakening

Throughout history, God has revealed himself to mankind through great seasons of revival. For example, the preaching ministry of John Wesley saw a harvest of countless souls into the Kingdom. The Azusa Street revival brought a fresh anointing of the Holy Spirit, manifested in the power of tongues. These revivals were remarkable and had a lasting impact on church history; however, many years ago, the Lord told me there wasn't going to be another revival like those we had known in the past. Instead, His next great move on the earth would be an awakening. Creation is asleep and has yet to be woken up.

The Renewal of the Mind

Genesis tells us that, in Eden, God put Adam to sleep to fashion Eve from his flesh. As a child of God, he had access to all the blessings in the heavenly realm; but he couldn't receive them while he was sleeping. It is not recorded anywhere in Scripture that God ever fully woke Adam—he never stepped into the fullness of those blessings. Unless somebody moved his body, Adam will awake in the same place.

Likewise, when we wake up, we're going to be in that same realm of Eden, the realm Adam went to sleep in. Eden is not a geographically located place, but a realm of blessing where everything is subdued to us, and there is overflow from the North, South, East and West. It has always been there, all around us—but we were asleep, and thus unable to access it.

Science suggests that we only use 10% of our brains. It has also been suggested that Einstein only used 11%. This means that for the average person, 90% of their brain is still asleep! People may disagree on the exact percentages, but I believe that 10% is right—because I believe God was the first tither. God breathed into Adam and woke up 10% of his brain. He wants to be reunited with Adam, who represents all of us, all of humankind. The Lord wants to be reunited with creation through the renewal of our minds. In fact, the Scripture encourages us that this is the method by which transformation comes – the renewal of the mind (Romans 12:2).

I believe God is preparing us. He wants us ready. He wants miracles and unseen realities to be our norm. People will touch our coats in a grocery store, and be healed. We will walk through hospitals and people will start getting up. We will sit down at a restaurant and bless the food and it will begin to multiply. We will say to a storm, "Peace" and it will be still. We will say to the lame, "Rise up and be healed," and in Jesus' name, it will be accomplished! How will we respond to the supernatural?

We know of Peter in the Bible, whose shadow healed the sick (Acts 5:15). We know of Paul's handkerchief that would heal anyone who came into contact with it (Acts 19:12). Imagine being in Peter's situation. Imagine walking like Paul walked. Are you going to be able to handle it? What are you going to do with yourself when you come into the fullness of who you really are? We need to prepare ourselves.

We went from being asleep in Adam to wearing the veil of the bride; but God is bringing forth a body—a son—that is one with Him. The Holy Ghost is our master teacher. He will lead us to a place, a realm called 'All truth'. I am eager for that awakening. Are you eager to see God in His fullness?

The Old Man and the New Man

On God's timetable, we are entering into the era of the Sabbath day. The Bible tells us that with the Lord, one day is as a thousand years, and a thousand years is as one day (2 Peter 3:8). There are about 4,000 years between Genesis and Christ. In God's time, this is 4 days. We see this pattern confirmed with the story of Lazarus, who had been dead for 4 days before the arrival of Jesus, who came to bring Him back to life (John 11:17). Likewise, creation had been dead for 4,000 years before the arrival of Christ, who came to bring it back to life. In the sight of the Lord 4,000 years is 4 days, and 4 days is 4,000 years.

From Christ until now, there are about 2,000 years—or 2 days. Taking the 4 days from Genesis to the arrival of Christ, and the 2 days that have passed since Christ, this adds up to 6 days. The first 6 days are over, and the Sabbath day has arrived. It is time for God to rest on the seventh day, the Sabbath. The only place it will be legal for God to rest is within man—the same man He created on the sixth day.

God has been working on that man—perfecting him—so that He can rest *in* Him on the Sabbath. If God is going to cease from His labor and turn the redemption of creation over to the sons of God, He needs a house to rest in. He cannot rest in something smaller than Himself. His desire is to rest in the house that He built. *We* are the new temple, the new house of God (1 Corinthians 3:16; 6:19). It's not the outside of man that God cares about; it's the inside, where He wants to dwell.

The day of man is over. The sixth day was necessary for a time, but it is over. We are entering *The Age of God*, where God rests within man. His rest can be seen in the embodiment of the sons of God. God chooses to express himself through His people. In order to make room for God, we have to let the new man (spirit) rule, and the old man (flesh) pass away. The new man is the one that has been born again. The old man is the flesh, the old nature that is passing away.

John the Baptist prepared the way for Jesus, saying, "He must increase, but I must decrease" (John 3:30). There is a decrease and an increase going on every day; that old man is

10

dying and the new man is being given life (see Romans 6; Ephesians 4; Colossians 3). As we die to ourselves and receive new life from Christ, our tastes change, we start to hang out in different places, different words capture our attention, and there is a progressive shift in our consciousness.

Many people find themselves connected to circumstances that are limiting. For some, old habits or cycles seem to control their existence. The acknowledgement of these things brings them face to face with their need for a deliverance—to be rescued or set free. Deliverance comes by speaking to the new man, and reminding the old man that he is dead. Listening to the old man will stall the process of growth. If we listen to the old man, he will keep us captive.

Some entire movements are built around the ministry of deliverance. They practice rituals that are expected to detach people from negative powers that influence or seem to control them. While this type of ministry serves a necessary place, I am convinced that lasting deliverance comes from a proper understanding and application of the life-giving Word of God. We receive deliverance by reminding ourselves that the old man is decreasing, and the new man is increasing. "Dying" is a word that adequately describes this process. We are dying to our old selves. We are changing forms. Christ has already defeated the second death for those in Him. We will never taste eternal death, but we are dying to ourselves every day. We are being given eternal life. Immortality is something we must learn to carry, something we learn to wear; and it changes the very cellular structures in our physical bodies (1 Corinthians 15:53-54). The more we cloth ourselves in the light of Christ, the more we are delivered, as the darkness of the old nature dissipates.

When the Scripture talks about Jesus being revealed, it talks about Him being revealed within a people. He cannot be revealed in a people unless there first be a "passing away." There is something passing away in you—that old man. "Therefore, if anyone is in Christ, he is a new creation; old things have passed away; behold, all things have become new" (2 Corinthians 5:17).

The Coming of the Son

Sometimes people get caught up with the idea of the rapture, with this whole idea of post-tribulation, mid-tribulation, and pre-tribulation. There are many different interpretations about how the last coming will unfold. The truth of the matter is that we are already "raised up" and made to sit together in heavenly places (Ephesians 2:6). But what does it mean when it says He will come again?

Jesus said that He would always be with us (Matthew 28:20); if this is true (and it is!), as so many *wait* on Him to return in a rapture, where is He coming from? Where has He been? How could He leave if He still resides in us? Jesus said that he would come like a thief in the night (Matthew 24:42-44). It is a different kind of coming He is talking about. He will come like a thief in the night to steal our old, raggedy, graveyard selves so that the new man will come forth. He is coming for our progression, growth, and maturity.

I personally believe that the specific time, days, and seasons of Christ's return are not important. As the sons, we are called to fellowship together, even amidst our differing beliefs about the consummation of the age. But we must realize that there has *already* been a rapture. We have been raised up and made to sit in heavenly places, in Christ. We walk in heavenly places *right now*. We are a chosen generation, a royal priesthood. Our citizenship is no longer of this temporal world, but of the heavens. There has been, and continues to be, an "ongoing rapture". Have you been left behind? Are you in the world but not of it? Have you received life in its fullness? Are you bringing light to the dark places? God is calling us and equipping us to be fully alive right now.

The Western Wall of the Temple in Jerusalem still stands. It is a beautiful remnant and symbol of God's faithfulness to Israel. But man could never build something that fully contains God. God is everywhere and always present. He declares:

> *Heaven is My throne,*
> *And earth is My footstool.*
> *What house will you build for Me?*
> —Acts 7:49

God will never come back and fill what man has built with mortar and brick. Paul tells us of another temple, a different temple made up of living stones. Jesus is the chief corner stone. *You* are the temple He is talking about (2 Corinthians 6:16).

In the days of Noah, they were eating, drinking, marrying and giving in marriage (Matthew 24:38). Life went on until Noah entered the Ark and the flood came and took them all away. Noah and his family were spared and given a new life—but, they didn't leave the earth. They inherited the earth (Genesis 8). Your old man is decreasing and the new man will remain. Your old nature is decreasing and your new nature is increasing. Your flesh is dying, and your spirit is being made alive—even while you remain in the flesh, on this earth.

The Revelation of the Son

What does it mean for the Son of Man to be revealed? It means that when the Son of Man is opened up, we will understand the mysteries and the secrets, and we will be able to see Him as He is. As Jesus said, "Even so will it be in the day when the son of man is *revealed*. In that day, he who is on the housetop, and his goods are in the house, let him not come down to take them away. And likewise the one who is in the field, let him not turn back" (Luke 17:30-31, emphasis added).

Remember what happened to Lot's wife? (See Genesis 19:26). The Kingdom of God is not fit for the one who takes hold of the plough and looks back (Luke 9:62). The old self likes to grab the plough and look back. Living in the flesh is self-defeating. When we choose this world over the heavens, we're spiritually blinded. We cannot perceive the fullness of God. All blessings are available to us now—we can't listen to the old man and rob ourselves of the fullness God has for us. Jesus completes and perfects that process. He is being revealed *in* our risen bodies, our transformed minds, and our new lives, long before He comes in the sky.

Jesus talked about this in the Bible. However, his words are often misunderstood. He said, "I tell you, in that night there will be two men in one bed: the one will be taken and the other will be left" (Luke 17:34). Was Jesus really referring to two men in bed together? If He were, His words would be totally misplaced. In that night there are two men—the old man and the new man—and one of them is taken. At the end of your night season, all that will remain is Christ in you, the hope of glory.

Jesus went on. He said there would be two women grinding at the mill (Luke 17:35). Throughout the Scriptures, women are representative of the soul. Psalm 34:2 says, "My soul shall make *her* boast in the Lord" (KJV, emphasis added). Again, the two women Jesus is talking about refer to the old soul and the new soul—one taken, one left. This is an on-going process.

Two men will be in the field (Luke 17:36). The field represents your mind. Right now it has tares and wheat in it, but God is in the process of dealing with the tares (see the Parable of the Wheat and the Tares, Matthew 13:24-30). We are coming to the fullness of understanding who we are and why we are here. The reference to two men in the field and one being taken represents the old mind that is decreasing and the new mind that is increasing. The old mind is dying and the new mind is being given life. We are looking and waiting for miracles. God is currently performing a miracle within your very mind! One day we will look back at ourselves and realize that there used to be two minds, two ways of thinking; but one is continually decreasing. We can put on the mind of Christ (1 Corinthians 2:16), and no longer be double-minded.

The concept of the antichrist is another misunderstood teaching. Paul said there were *many* antichrists in his day, not just one (1 John 2:18). The Greek word translated as "anti" does not mean *against*; it means *instead of.* There are many antichrists present in this world, because there are many things that we put over and above Christ. We choose worldly things in place of godly things. We choose talent, instead of the anointing. We focus on external appearance instead of the heart. We choose to be selfish instead of generous. We choose religion instead of relationship. We listen to the words of the old man instead of the Word of the Lord. We put our thoughts and ways above His thoughts and ways. For too long, all of these things have been consistently chosen *instead of* God.

Which man are you listening to—the old man or the new man? Which woman are you feeding, the old woman or the new woman? Where are you in your life? As a man thinks, so is he (Proverbs 23:7). The Scriptures tell us in Philippians 2:5-7: "Let this mind be in you which was also in Christ Jesus, who, being in the form of God, did not consider it robbery to be equal with God, but made Himself of no reputation, taking the form of a bondservant, and coming in the likeness of men." We are to put on the very mind of Christ—who contained the fullness of God Almighty, yet chose to humble

16

Himself as a man, even to the point of death! (Philippians 2:8). What will it look like if we—mortals made from the dust of the earth—put on the very mind of Christ?

God intends to empty you out and deposit Himself in you, so that it is no longer you who lives, but Him. Then we can confidently proclaim, "If you have seen me, you have seen the Father!" We are becoming the visible expression of an invisible God. He desires to be seen *in* a people. His desire is for the new man—not the old *and* new man—to walk with him in the *cool* of the day—or in the *spirit* of the day (Genesis 3:8). We're here to be conformed into the image of the beloved Son.

If we desire to be set free and no longer held captive by the old man, then there are some beliefs that we need to dispel. The next chapter deals with the lies we often believe, which hinder our growth in God. Truth will renew our minds and make us free.

Chapter 2
Lies of the Enemy

As human beings, we are equipped with five natural senses: the ability to see, feel, touch, taste, and smell. It is through these senses that our flesh, or lower nature, seeks to deceive us. The "lies of the enemy" often seek to use our own perceptions against us. They are perverted so that we do not see clearly or hear clearly. If we allow ourselves to get distracted by our senses—what we see, feel, touch, taste, and smell—the result is that we walk in darkness. Satan best operates in this realm, and takes advantage of our natural weakness in this area.

The Deception of Our Senses

Adam and Eve got in trouble in the garden because they "knew" good and evil through their senses. Genesis 3:6 says, "So when the woman saw that the tree was good for food, that it was pleasant to the eyes, and a tree desirable to make one wise, she took of its fruit and ate. She also gave to her husband with her, and he ate."

She *listened* to the serpent. She saw that the fruit *looked* good. So she *touched* it and *tasted* it. What she experienced through her body affected the judgement of her mind. Instead of seeing through eyes of faith, Adam and Eve were persuaded by what they physically saw and heard.

Our senses *seem* logical and reliable to us. The Word of God says that once we have our senses exercised, only then can we *discern* good and evil (Hebrews 5:14). When you discern, you are able to distinguish between fact and falsehood. When we learn to *discern* through the Spirit rather than seeking to *know* by the intellect, strongholds are broken down. Our minds are renewed. When we discern good and evil rather than know it by the intellect, we realize that all things really do work together for good (Romans 8:28).

The minds of people are distorted due to our carnal nature and understanding. Below we will look at the true differences between the devil and man. We will take the devil out of heaven and return him to the earth where he belongs. But first we must clarify some oft-misunderstood Scriptures.

The Progression of the Fall

Traditional biblical interpretation has taught us that, according to Genesis, in the Garden of Eden man fell from his rightful place or position in God because of disobedience. When God placed Adam and Eve in the garden, He gave them clear boundaries concerning what they did or did not have

20

access to. They crossed those boundaries by eating of a tree that had been forbidden, and the consequence of that decision is commonly referred to as the "fall of man".

While this is an accurate summary of what took place in the garden to lead to man's loss of dominion, it is important to note that the "fall" itself wasn't a singular incident. There were actually three "falls," or to say it another way, there were three progressive parts to the fall. The first two falls were not equivalent to sin entering the world; but they set the stage for the third and final fall, which was the eating of the forbidden fruit. After the third fall, sin entered the world and God had to send Adam and Eve away from the Garden. The third fall was the culmination of the first two, showing the progressive nature of sin. Adam and Eve didn't arbitrarily decide to sin one day—there were previous "falls" that allowed them to go down this path.

Anything *outside* of God is of a fallen nature. The minute God blew Adam outside of Himself in Genesis 2:7, Adam started falling. For the sake of clarity in explanation, we will call that the first part of the fall. Being outside of God holds the potential of us choosing to reject Him. Now, you might wonder, "Why would God spit Adam outside of Himself in the first place?" God had the intent of bringing Adam back into Himself. God sensed something flawed in Adam. Something needed refining. Part of His redemptive plan was to release Adam from Himself so that Adam would learn to walk as God; then reunite with the new Adam in a state of total oneness (Romans 8:20).

When Adam was in God, Eve was in Adam. Therefore, there was neither male nor female. When Adam was put in the garden, Eve was inside of him. They were one. The moment Adam felt like he needed something *besides* God, he fell further. After God created Adam He said, "It is not good that man should be alone..." (Genesis 2:18). God sensed Adam's aloneness. Adam felt that Eve had to be revealed even though he already had fellowship with God. Adam needed something besides God. That was the second part of the fall. Consequently, God took Eve from inside of Adam and created male and female.

The second fall and the third fall make up the first difference between man and the devil. *Man* fell from heaven, not the devil. Contrary to what we have heard in the past, I don't believe that the devil was ever in heaven. The realm of dominion and power and oneness in *Eden* is the realm from which Adam fell. Initially, Adam was with God, walking with Him in the cool of the day. The devil was never in fellowship with God. You might have an issue with this, but just hang on, let us look at the big picture.

When Eve took the fruit that God had told them not to eat, it was Eve who was deceived and not Adam (1 Timothy 2:14). Eve, the first female created, symbolizes the Church. Adam, as the first male created, represents Christ. Eve is the bride of Adam, just as the Church is the bride of Christ. Adam was participating in a larger plan in a way similar to that of Christ. Jesus tasted of the death realm for His woman, for the Church; Adam tasted of the death realm for his woman, who was Eve.

22

Adam was not deceived, he ate to cover Eve. Jesus was not deceived, he ate to cover the bride. He ate to cover *you*. Adam knew the plan of God in Christ. Adam went along with something that was far older than himself. Adam had an inclination to the ancient understanding that if he tasted death and sin, it would enable him to cover the woman, just as Jesus tasted death and sin in order to cover the Church.

> "For the creation was subjected to futility, not willingly, but because of Him who subjected it in hope; because the creation itself also will be delivered from the bondage of corruption into the glorious liberty of the children of God."
>
> —Romans 8:20-21

Creation, including us, was made subject to vanity and sin— not willingly, but by reason of hope. What does that mean? Adam—man—was made subject to sin, not of his own will, but by the greater hope that if God spit man out of Himself, He could bring a new man back into Himself. Man could be one with God again. This is God's plan. He had already slain the lamb *before* the foundation to cover Adam's sin (John 17:24; Ephesians 1:4; 1 Peter 1:20).

Who is Lucifer?

One of the most commonly misinterpreted names in Scripture is the reference to Lucifer. His name has been villainized to the extent that he is traditionally understood as synonymous with the devil or Satan. What is interesting, however, is that Lucifer is never mentioned in reference to the devil, or Satan, nor is he even mentioned with the serpent. The name Lucifer is mentioned once throughout the entire Bible, all by itself. Isaiah 14:12 says, "How you are fallen from heaven, O Lucifer, son of the morning! How you are cut down to the ground, You who weakened the nations!"

Why have we studied Lucifer in connection with the devil, the ancient serpent, Satan, and all the demons? Why do we take the liberty to group Lucifer with the devil? Because we have eyes that don't see, and ears that don't hear. The Scripture says the word Lucifer means "light bearer." The light bearer was Adam who walked with God in the cool of the day before he fell. Adam was the one who bore the light. Adam was the one that fell. Adam was the one that was kicked out of Eden. Adam was the one who started out walking in the Spirit with God, in the cool of the day, before he decided that he wanted to do his own thing.

Lucifer is Adam. Isaiah continues:

> For you have said in your heart:
> "I will ascend into heaven,
> I will exalt my throne above the stars of God;
> I will also sit on the mount of the
> congregation
> On the farthest sides of the north;
> I will ascend above the heights of the clouds,
> I will be like the Most High."
> Yet you shall be brought down to Sheol,

To the lowest depths of the Pit.

—Isaiah 14:13-14

In the first part of the passage it says, "...you have said in your *heart*" (emphasis added). Adam's heart is part of his soul realm. We know that Eve is the expression of the soulish realm of man. She embodies the heart and soul of Adam. Eve was deceived, and ate the fruit. Adam, by choosing to come into agreement with Eve, covered her and fell with her. He took on her mindset by eating the fruit. Adam and Eve are one, and thus, inseparable. When Adam fell, he encompassed Eve. Together they represent the fallen state of humanity. Therefore when the Scripture speaks of Lucifer, it speaks of the mindset of Adam, Eve, and all of fallen humanity.

Adam's decision was not one of ignorance; in fact, he knew exactly what he was doing. By his action he wanted to be like God, knowing good and evil. By coming into agreement with Eve, Adam rivaled God's own authority. The devil tempted Eve by saying, "...God knows that in the day you eat of it your eyes will be opened, and you will be like God, *knowing* good and evil" (Genesis 3:5, emphasis added). When Adam took the fruit from Eve, he took on that mindset. He exalted himself above God. Adam was effectively saying: "I'm going to be my own God. I am going to ascend into heaven. I do not care what God says. I'm going to be like God, while not being *in* God. I'm going to do it all on my own, apart from Him."

By saying this, Lucifer—or Adam—was falling down to a lower realm of life. The passage goes on:

25

Those who see you will gaze at you,
And consider you, saying:
"Is this the *man* who made the earth tremble,
Who shook kingdoms,
Who made the world as a wilderness
And destroyed its cities,
Who did not open the house of his
prisoners?"

—Isaiah 14:16-17 (emphasis added)

Is this the *man* who made the earth to tremble? (verse 16). The verse doesn't talk about the devil, Satan, demons, snakes, leopards, or lions; it says "Is this the man?" Lucifer was a man. Is this the man who made the earth to tremble, shook the kingdoms, and made the world as a wilderness? Is this the *man* responsible for the downfall of this world? Yes...*man!*

Who is the King of Tyre?

Ezekiel 28 refers to one, the King of Tyre. This reference is commonly associated with Satan. However, the description seems to be more in line with the characteristics of *Lucifer*, and therefore Adam. God makes a proclamation against the King of Tyre, saying:

...your heart is lifted up,
And you say, 'I am a god,
I sit in the seat of gods,
In the midst of the seas,'
Yet you are a *man*, and not a god,

> Though you set your heart as the heart of a
> god...
>
> —Ezekiel 28:2 (emphasis added)

The proclamation continues in verses 12-13:

> You were the seal of perfection,
> Full of wisdom and perfect in beauty.
> You were in Eden, the garden of God;
> Every precious stone was your covering:
> The sardius, topaz, and diamond,
> Beryl, onyx, and jasper,
> Sapphire, turquoise, and emerald with gold.
> The workmanship of your timbrels and pipes
> Was prepared for you on the day you were
> created.

The spirit of the King of Tyre is associated with Adam. Adam was the one who fell from the heavenly realm of Eden. The precious stones that were covering the King of Tyre represent the priesthood. The Old Testament tells us that the same stones covered the breastplate of the high priest. Compare the similarities of Ezekiel and Exodus—the passage describes the making of the breastplate:

> And they set in it four rows of stones: a row
> with a sardius, a topaz, and an emerald was
> the first row; the second row, a turquoise, a
> sapphire, and a diamond; the third row, a
> jacinth, an agate, and an amethyst; the fourth
> row, a beryl, an onyx, and a jasper. They were

enclosed in settings of gold in their mountings. There were twelve stones according to the names of the sons of Israel: according to their names, engraved like a signet, each one with its own name according to the twelve tribes.

—Exodus 39:10-14

The New Jerusalem in Revelation 21—which is the glorious bride, the consecrated Church—is adorned with many of these same stones. The stones represent a royal priesthood, a chosen generation; they represent us. Even though we fell, God wants us back in the garden; even greater than that, God wants us to *become* His garden.

Three Realms of Heaven

We have seen that heaven cannot possibly be linked to the devil. The devil was not in heaven. Traditional teaching may negate this view by appealing to certain Scriptures that seem to connect heaven with the devil, such as Revelation 12:7-9: "And war broke out in heaven: Michael and his angels fought with the dragon; and the dragon and his angels fought, but they did not prevail, nor was a place found for them in heaven any longer. So the great dragon was cast out, that serpent of old, called the Devil and Satan, who deceives the whole world; he was cast to the earth, and his angels were cast out with him."

Before jumping to conclusions, let us recognize what the word "heaven" means here. The Bible talks about three types of "heavens," or three realms of heaven. The first heaven alludes to the visible realm of the atmosphere where Satan has influence. He is the prince of the power of the air (Ephesians 2:1-2). Satan is the god of this system, bound to this realm. This is where the battle of Revelation 12 took place.

The second heaven represents the mind of man. Ephesians talks about man's battle against Satan in the mind, "against spiritual hosts of wickedness in the heavenly places" (Ephesians 6:12). Jesus spoke of man's authority to influence what happens "in heaven." He said, "Assuredly, I say to you, whatever you bind on earth will be bound in heaven, and whatever you loose on earth will be loosed in heaven" (Matthew 18:18). In other words, when we discern by the Spirit and reject Satan's influence in the realm of our minds, he is bound; he cannot sway us. But when we give attention to Satan without guarding our hearts and minds, his influence is loosed upon our minds. We are deceived. When Eve listened to Satan in the Garden of Eden, she subjected her mind to a lesser law. Satan was already loosed in the first heaven, but man gave Satan access to—or influence over—the second heaven: the mind of man.

The apostle Paul speaks of the third heaven. He says, "I know a man in Christ who fourteen years ago—whether in the body I do not know, or whether out of the body I do not know, God knows—such a one was caught up to the third heaven. And I know such a man—whether in the body or out of the body I do not know, God knows—how he was caught up into Paradise and heard inexpressible words, which it is not lawful for a man to utter" (2 Corinthians 12:2-4). This third heaven is the highest realm where God dwells, the Kingdom of heaven.

When we speak of man falling from heaven, we are specifically talking about the third heaven. This is the realm where man fell from, and will be restored to. Satan cannot access the third heaven. He never was, and never will be, permitted to enter this heaven. Evil cannot enter in. We know that Satan was a liar and a murderer *from the beginning* (John 8:44). Therefore, he could never have existed in this realm. All of these Scriptural insights lead us to the first difference between man and the devil.

The First Difference: Man fell from heaven, not the devil.

We may never agree on doctrine, but we can come into the unity of the faith. Indeed, we *will* come into the unity of the faith. No matter how you look at it, we come to the same conclusion. Whether Adam fell when he was breathed out of God, when he ate the fruit as a covering for Eve, or when he ate of it to ascend to heaven and be like God without God, we are left with the same conclusion. Man fell and needs to be reunited with God. Adam "left" God. God never left Adam.

If you believe that the devil was in heaven with God, it will affect your discernment; it will affect your vision because it puts the devil in a place of authority. It puts him in a place of being like God, or like *a* god. This type of thinking puts the devil up on a pedestal next to God. It will cause your vision to be distorted.

What does it look like when we put Satan back in his place? What happens when we guard our minds by the Spirit, and rightly understand the power of God in contrast to the weakness of the enemy? How will we operate? Luke 10 gives us a vivid description of the experience of the seventy that Jesus sent out:

> Then the seventy returned with joy, saying, "Lord, even the demons are subject to us in Your name." And He said to them, "I saw Satan fall like lightning from heaven. Behold, I give you the authority to trample on serpents and scorpions, and over all the power of the enemy, and nothing shall by any means hurt you."
>
> —Luke 10:17-19

Jesus says Satan fell from heaven like lightning. References to light in the Scripture often refer to revelation and understanding. He is talking about the fall of Lucifer's mindset, of the carnal mind of man. Our revelation of Satan is falling. The less we acknowledge the devil, the more his influence diminishes, and he falls from our consciousness. Only when we take Satan out of heaven in our minds, will we experience success in battle against him.

Believing Satan is like God affects your senses. The Scriptures say, "He who has ears to hear, let him hear" (Matthew 11:15). Satan is not a god and he is not all-powerful. You belittle God when you believe that Satan was in heaven with God, rebelled against God in heaven, and God consequently had to

31

fight in order to keep His own kingdom. Do you believe that Satan had a chance at winning—because by the time God found out and got to Satan, he had already turned a third of the angels against God? Do you believe that God could have been slow, even in His own heaven? It is a lie out of the pit of hell that will affect how you hear the Gospel, and it will affect your relationship with God.

The Second Difference: The devil did not fall with a third of the angels. It was man who fell.

Another lie is that a third of the angels fell together with Satan. Revelation 12:3-4a says, "And another sign appeared in heaven: behold, a great, fiery red dragon having seven heads and ten horns, and seven diadems on his heads. His tail drew a third of the stars of heaven and threw them to the earth."

People often falsely assume that the third of the stars that fell from heaven are fallen angels. No matter what kind of angel it is, there is no being that has enough nerve to rebel against God in His own heaven. Moreover, if the angels and Satan were in heaven as sinful beings, then it would be unlawful for man to have to get born again to go to heaven. If the angels and Satan were in heaven while they had sin, then why could not you and I go to heaven with sin?

I believe that the "one third" of fallen stars refers to a third of man. You are spirit, soul, and body (1 Thessalonians 5:23). The soul fell. A third of you fell with Adam. The soul encompasses our mind, will, and emotions, which became tainted and thus, in need of redemption. Satan's deception caused the soul of man to fall, followed by the spirit and body.

The Third Difference: The devil is completely evil, but man can be both good and evil.

The Purpose of the Devil

There is a lie out there that everything bad is caused by the devil. But the Bible tells us otherwise: "And we know that all things work together for good to those who love God, to those who are the called according to His purpose" (Romans 8:28).

If all things work together for good, God is in control. The devil is an instrument in God's hands. God is a master quilt-maker, stitching together a patchwork of squares—incorporating both light and dark pieces—but the ultimate story He weaves is one of redemption. Although the journey may not always look and feel "good," the Lord is leading His people to a glorious destiny.

Scripture teaches that God formed the light and created darkness.

> That they may know from the rising of the
> sun to its setting
> That there is none besides Me.
> I am the LORD, and there is no other;
> I form the light and create darkness,
> I make peace and create calamity;

I, the LORD, have created it.

—Isaiah 45:6-7

He formed the light and created evil; He created the smiths man to blow upon the coals, in order to prepare a vessel for His use (Isaiah 54:16). God uses negative and positive, light and darkness, to process us. Paul explains: "In this you greatly rejoice, though now for a little while, if need be, you have been grieved by various trials, that the genuineness of your faith, being much more precious than gold that perishes, though it is tested by fire, may be found to praise, honor, and glory at the revelation of Jesus Christ..." (1 Peter 1:6-7). I love the fact that God is that big!

It is through trials and testing that we are purified and become visible expressions of Christ. We are being chipped away and chipped away until the image of the Holy God is perfectly formed inside of us. Even if being chiseled, hammered, and put through fire doesn't feel good—don't be so quick to give Satan the credit. The Lord is in control, and He can use even something that doesn't seem "good" to bring about change in His people, and glory and honor to Himself. Satan's plans can't hold a candle to the consuming fire of God's glory and holiness. He is the master potter.

Did the devil not go to God for permission before he did certain things? In the story of Job, the devil had to receive God's consent before tempting Job (Job 1:11-12). We have made the devil so big that we imagine he competes with God Himself—yet he is only an instrument. He is not omnipresent. He is a created being. He was a liar and murderer from the *beginning* (John 8:44). God is God all by Himself. There is none beside Him!

Psalms tells us:

> Lord, You have been our dwelling place in all
> generations.
> Before the mountains were brought forth,
> Or ever You had formed the earth and the
> world,
> Even from everlasting to everlasting, You are
> God.
>
> —Psalm 90:1-2

Satan could never be like God. He is a fool for trying, and we are foolish to give him more credit than he deserves.

People sometimes live and think as if the devil is after them, trying to harm them, or kill them—but he does not have that much power. He was created to fulfill his limited role, and cannot do whatever he pleases. The Scriptures say God has set the borders; He has set the borders on the oceans, the waters, the moon, the sun and the stars. God has put the seasons in place and designates everything to happen according to its time (Proverbs 8:22-31; Job 38; Psalm 104). When it comes to the devil, is God all of the sudden powerless? Would He allow Satan to run rampant on the earth?

When you hold to the belief that everything that looks bad is from the devil, it will affect your sense of discernment. It will affect your vision. You cannot walk according to your own faulty reasoning or knowledge. You have to walk by faith. Paul said, "I am crucified with Christ: nevertheless I live; yet not I, but Christ liveth in me: and the life which I now live in the flesh I live by the *faith* of the Son of God, who loved me, and gave himself for me" (Galatians 2:20, KJV, emphasis added).

The Battle within Man

Unlike the devil who was evil from the beginning, man can display a combination of both good and evil. Consider the Scriptures listed below:

> Galatians 3:22-25: "But the Scripture has confined all under sin, that the promise by faith in Jesus Christ might be given to those who believe. But *before faith came*, we were kept under guard by the law, kept for the faith which would afterward be revealed. Therefore the law was our tutor to bring us to Christ, that we might be justified by faith. But *after faith has come*, we are no longer under a tutor" (emphasis added).

> Romans 7:21-23: "I find then a law, that, when I would do good, evil is present with me. For I delight in the law of God after the inward man: But I see another law in my members, warring against the law of my mind,

and bringing me into captivity to the law of sin which is in my members" (KJV).

Romans 8:5-8: "For those who live according to the flesh set their minds on the things of the flesh, but those who live according to the Spirit, the things of the Spirit. For to be carnally minded is death, but to be spiritually minded is life and peace. Because the carnal mind is enmity against God; for it is not subject to the law of God, nor indeed can be. So then, those who are in the flesh cannot please God."

Man has the ability to display two natures. For those in Christ, their old nature is dying and their new nature is being given life, by the power of the Spirit. For those living according to the flesh, the old man still has influence in their thoughts, minds, and actions. Satan can take advantage of this by encouraging the old man. But for those with a renewed mind, a new Spirit is given. We must choose to not walk after the flesh but instead to yield to the Spirit.

The devil is real. He is out there, but most of the trouble you get in is because of you—because you have two personalities, so to speak. You have an old man and a new man. The old man, who is supposed to be crucified with Christ, is the one acting up in your life. It is the old man that has a tendency to lean toward the old mindset, not the devil. The old man is decreasing and the new man is increasing.

You need to grasp the fact that sometimes the evil that happens in your life is because of the old man in you. Therefore, you need to deal with him so that the new man will increase. We will talk about him in detail in proceeding chapters.

The Fourth Difference: The devil does not have dominion of this earth. Man does.

Another lie of the devil is that Adam gave the title deed of the earth to Satan—but this never happened. Adam never owned the earth, so it was never his to give away. God gave Adam *dominion* over creation, but he did not have ownership (Gen 1:26).

Psalm 24:1 says:

> The earth is the LORD'S, and all its fullness,
> The world and those who dwell therein.

Therefore, when Scripture talks about Satan being the god of this world, it means that Satan has influence in an age, a system, a limited amount of time, or a dispensation. He is not the god of the earth because the earth does not belong to him. The earth is the Lord's and God wants us to have dominion over His earth. Let's put Satan back in his place!

In Genesis, we read that Satan was cursed as a snake crawling on his belly in the dirt (Genesis 3:14). Yet somehow in Revelation 12:3, we discover that he is a dragon. How did he suddenly transform into a dragon? Somewhere between the first and last pages of the Bible—between the beginning and end of time as we know it—Satan gained power. How is this so? Satan feeds off of the power that humans give him. We have prophesied him into our schools, government, and politics. We have allowed him and given him permission to go in to these areas. We put him in the heavens. God confined him to the dust of the earth, but we exalted him to heaven.

God decreed that Satan would crawl on the earth on his belly and eat the dust of the ground (Genesis 3:14). In other words, his food would be the carnality, the dustiness, or the fleshliness of man. The sin nature is referred to as the flesh or fleshly nature. As we begin to put away the flesh, as the flesh decreases, it leaves less and less a space for the serpent to crawl. Let's not make him all-powerful, when he isn't. God has set the borders, not Satan.

The great dragon will be cast down when you begin to put away the flesh. The great dragon and his thoughts and ideas will be cast down from having control of your mind. But woe to those who are still in their flesh, who live in the earth realm where the devil still has a place. Glory to God who says that his time is short! (Revelation 12:12). The dragon has only a short time because the Creator God is in control—always!

Believing that Adam gave the earth to the devil will affect your life, reasoning, and destiny. We have been given dominion over the earth. He has promised the "ends of the earth" for our possession (Psalm 2:8).

The Fifth Difference: Man is spirit, soul, and body; the devil is a principality and power.

39

Man consists of spirit, soul, and body. "Now may the God of peace Himself sanctify you completely; and may your whole *spirit, soul,* and *body* be preserved blameless at the coming of our Lord Jesus Christ" (1 Thessalonians 5:23, emphasis added).

Satan on the other hand, can be identified as a principality, power, or negative energy source. Paul exhorts us: "Put on the whole armor of God, that you may be able to stand against the wiles of the devil. For we do not wrestle against flesh and blood, but against principalities, against powers, against the rulers of the darkness of this age, against spiritual hosts of wickedness in the heavenly places" (Ephesians 6:11-12).

Satan does not have arms, feet, or bodily forms, because he is an energy source. Satan is an understanding, not flesh and blood. If you believe he is anything else, it will affect how you hear God. He is a messenger that likes to agree with the old man, old nature, the mind of flesh, or the natural man. He tries to influence us by resurrecting our old, dying nature, so that we start to question the validity of our new nature, which is being given life through Christ. We must give the devil no place!

We need to realize that we war not against flesh and blood, but against doctrines, thoughts, principalities, and powers. Satan tried to tempt Jesus by appealing to thoughts, wills, and emotions. Jesus responded each time by saying "It is written…" (Matthew 4:1-11). He appealed directly to God's Word and never addressed the devil. He kept only the Word of God in His heart and in His mouth, giving the devil no attention. We can gain much wisdom by looking at Jesus' response to Satan's temptations. Don't misjudge the battleground by trying to fight back in the flesh. The real battle takes place in your mind.

Paul writes in Corinthians:

But as it is written:

"Eye has not seen, nor ear heard,
Nor have entered into the heart of man
The things which God has prepared for those who love Him."
But God has revealed them to us through His Spirit. For the Spirit searches all things, yes, the deep things of God.
—1 Corinthians 2:9-10

He continues in verse 13: "These things we also speak, not in words which man's wisdom teaches but which the Holy Spirit teaches, comparing spiritual things with spiritual. But the natural man does not receive the things of the Spirit of God, for they are foolishness to him; nor can he know them, because they are spiritually discerned" (1 Corinthians 2:13-14).

Paul tells us that the *natural man* cannot receive the things of God. Our new man is able to hear and understand God. We learn by discernment through the Spirit. We fight not according to the flesh, but by our renewed minds received through the Spirit. The battle, then, lies in silencing the old man, so that the new man can flourish. The struggle lies within. There are two manners of men in you—an old man that is passing away, and a new man who expresses life. We are so busy fighting the devil on the outside that we forget our true enemy—the old man on the inside! Just as Jesus cleansed the Temple in Jerusalem by freeing it of the moneychangers, it is time for us to clean the inside of the true Temple...you!

Chapter 3
Wrestling with the Truth

Imagine that you are watching a wrestling match. The referee blows his whistle, signaling the start of the match. You expect to see one guy pitted against the other, each looking for an opportunity to take his opponent down. Instead, you watch in amazement as one of the guys turns his back to his opponent and begins fighting an imaginary enemy. His attention is drawn away from the real match. The other guy quickly takes advantage of this development, pinning his opponent in an instant, while his back is turned.

If you don't recognize the true battle, there is no way that you will win!

Jacob's Wrestling Match

In Genesis 32, we come across the story of Jacob sending his whole family ahead of him just before meeting Esau. In verse 22 he "crossed over the ford of Jabbok." The Hebrew name

Jabbok *means to empty out.* Jacob emptied out his whole household: his wives, his kids, and all of his possessions. He emptied himself completely—of all external, natural, and physical connections.

Verse 23 continues: "He took them, sent them over the brook, and sent over what he had. Then Jacob was left alone..." Suddenly, there was only Jacob. There is some hidden truth here. When the Scripture says that Jacob was left alone, I believe that this was the season Jacob wrestled with himself.

Some people say that Jacob wrestled with an angel, and some people say it was God. However, if it was God or the angels, couldn't they easily whip Jacob? Did it really take God all night to beat him? Would a man's strength rival that of an angel's, or the Lord Himself? God does not wrestle. He could snap his finger and you would be out of here. God is not going to wrestle with you. The angels are not going to wrestle with you. You will be left alone to wrestle with yourself!

Let's take a closer look at the encounter. Verse 24 goes on:

> Then Jacob was left alone; and a *Man* wrestled with him until the breaking of day. Now when He saw that He did not prevail against him, He touched the socket of his hip; and the socket of Jacob's hip was out of joint as He wrestled with him. And He said, "Let Me go, for the day breaks."

—Genesis 32:24-26 (emphasis added)

The Scripture tells us that the man touched Jacob's *socket*, not his hip. The socket is located on the inside, not the outside. Jacob was touched on the inside, indicating an internal work. He was being changed from the inside out. The passage continues:

> But he said, "I will not let You go unless You bless me!"
>
> So He said to him, "What is your name?" He said, "Jacob."
>
> And He said, "Your name shall no longer be called Jacob, but Israel; for you have struggled with God and with men, and have prevailed."
> —Genesis 32:26-28

A name change signifies a nature change. Jacob literally means *liar* or *supplanter*. Jacob's name was changed to Israel, which means *father of nations*.

"For you have struggled with God and with man and have prevailed" (Genesis 32:28). Jacob wrestled with himself. Hence he struggled with God in the sense that he struggled with grasping God's purpose, which can only be revealed and understood through the new mind. He prevailed not in overcoming God, but in realizing the truth, and seeing the need to let the new man rule and defeat the old man. You

45

also are in need of a nature change so that the old man in you is defeated and the new man takes control.

> Then Jacob asked, saying, "Tell me Your name, I pray."
>
> And He said, "Why is it that you ask about My name?" And He blessed him there.
>
> —Genesis 32:24-29

Jacob was asking him about his nature, not simply his name. Jacob knew it was a supernatural encounter, and not a physical encounter.

This encounter perfectly describes submission of the flesh to the Spirit. The whole point was for Jacob to realize that he was wrestling with himself. God wanted Jacob to realize that he was his only enemy. There are situations where blessing comes from the most unlikely sources. When the natural, old man submits to the spirit-man, there will always be pronounced blessing!

Your Wrestling Match

Are you wrestling with the truth? Don't be distracted by the devil; what he does is irrelevant. Concentrate on your old self that is still wrestling with the revelation. Paul talked about the war going on in his members. He says, "For what I am doing, I do not understand. For what I will to do, that I do not practice; but what I hate, that I do" (Romans 7:15).

He continues in verse 21:

> I find then a law, that, when I would do good,
> evil is present with me. For I delight in the law
> of God after the inward man: But I see
> another law in my members, warring against
> the law of my mind, and bringing me into
> captivity to the law of sin which is in my
> members. O wretched man that I am! who
> shall deliver me from the body of this death? I
> thank God through Jesus Christ our Lord. So
> then with the mind I myself serve the law of
> God; but with the flesh the law of sin.
> —Romans 7:21-25, KJV

There is a man inside the temple of our bodies, trying to be God. He wants to be the god of the temple. He wants to do whatever he wants, go wherever he pleases, and say whatever he likes. Are you living like this? Do you live in subjection to the flesh, or to the Spirit? There are only two choices. This struggle describes the old and new man battling for control. Paul recognized the war happening within himself.

Remember what we are fighting against. The Scripture tells us, "For we do not wrestle against flesh and blood, but against principalities, against powers, against the rulers of the darkness of this age, against spiritual hosts of wickedness in the heavenly places" (Ephesians 6:12). We don't wrestle against flesh and blood; we aren't struggling with anything in the natural. The battle is not against the devil. We struggle with what's inside.

We wrestle against *principalities* and *powers*. That word *principalities* deals with principles, and *powers* deals with doctrine. We wrestle with our own thoughts and ideas. God is telling us to focus not on the external, but on the internal. Our job is to deal with ourselves. The battle is fought within.

Repairing the Breach

Jacob called the name of the place where he struggled Peniel (Genesis 32:30). But did you know that there is a Pineal gland in your head? Now Peniel and Pineal are different places; Peniel is a geographically located place, and the pineal gland sits right in the middle of the brain between the two hemispheres. Scientists don't yet know the full extent of its function. They know that it reacts to light and helps regulate your circadian rhythm. It releases the hormone melatonin in response to waking and sleeping patterns, which are dictated by daylight and darkness. When the pineal gland is activated, the brain transitions from a state of sleeping to a state of wakefulness, giving it the common nickname "third eye." It functions like an eye ball, has the liquid of an eye ball, and even contains a retina. Many researchers connect the pineal gland with the supernatural, and believe that it enables people to move in the spirit realm. It is what allows us to truly see.

There is a breach that divides the two sides of the brain. The left side of the brain is where logic, facts, mathematics, and analytical thinking takes place. The right side of the brain is characterized by creativity, art, and intuitive thinking. It has been proven that most people have a dominant side and use one more than the other.

The Scripture mentions a generation that will repair the breach. Isaiah 58 talks about Israel falling short and not truly knowing or delighting in their God. But then the Lord contrasts this picture with the arrival of a new generation that would surpass the failings of their ancestors. The Scripture says:

> The Lord will guide you continually,
> And satisfy your soul in drought,
> And strengthen your bones;
> You shall be like a watered garden,
> And like a spring of water, whose waters do not fail.
> Those from among you
> Shall build the old waste places;
> You shall raise up the foundations of many generations;
> And you shall be called the *Repairer of the Breach*,
> The Restorer of Streets to Dwell In.
> —Isaiah 58:11-12 (emphasis added)

I believe that when that breach is repaired, both sides of the brain will be activated. We will then be able to move where we are meant to move, live where we are supposed to live, and see what we are supposed to see. That is why we are so hungry for the supernatural—because it is supposed to be a part of our everyday lives. The supernatural will become the new normal, our normal mode of operation.

Pineal is a realm. Jacob walked across a place called Peniel. I believe this new generation will be awakened when the Holy Ghost walks across your Pineal gland. It will begin to awaken you to who you are supposed to be and what you are predestined to do. Our "third eye" will be opened by the Holy Spirit.

When Jacob went away from his encounter, the Bible says he walked with a limp (Genesis 32:31). The King James Version uses the word "halt." This means that he never went anywhere again without a hesitation. Everywhere he went, he remembered that it was not his will to be done, but God's. From that moment on, he never did just what *he* wanted to do. He hesitated before he walked because his desire was to stay in the will of God.

Be careful before jumping to conclusions, beloved, because you may be your own worst enemy!

The Tongue

God has set borders on everything because He is God. There are built-in limitations. The devil cannot invent anything. He cannot come up with anything new. His main activity is to try to turn you against yourself. We know about the devil and we know he is coming and going—but he is just not as busy and as smart as the Church has professed him to be.

We need to realize the truth about him. We need to go into the temple and clean it out, like Jesus did—the temple being our inner man. We need to clean out our whole house—the money changers, those that buy and sell doves, and those that make merchandise of the Holy Ghost or the gifts of the Holy Spirit (Matthew 21:12). We need to go into the temple and clean it out, and cause it to be what God intended for it to be—a house of prayer and a house of communion. Our very bodies are to be a house of oneness where we meet and agree and mesh with God. Hallelujah!

We must stop giving credit to the devil, and focus on our true enemy *within*. James tells us, "And the tongue is a fire, a world of iniquity. The tongue is so set among our members that it defiles the whole body, and sets on fire the course of nature; and it is set on fire by hell" (James 3:6). He is referencing the *tongue*—not hell, and not the devil—but a member of our own bodies. The tongue is so influential among our members that it defiles the *whole* body. There is no need for the devil to step in, because we are doing his job all on our own.

The tongue sets on fire the course of nature and is set on fire by hell. Hell is not only a geographically located place; it is a realm in which the tongue is found. If you really want to spend a season in hell, let somebody crucify you with their words. The tongue has the ability to manifest the experience and mindset of hell itself.

James continues:

> For every kind of beast and bird, of reptile
> and creature of the sea, is tamed and has
> been tamed by mankind. But no man can
> tame the tongue. It is an unruly evil, full of
> deadly poison. With it we bless our God and
> Father, and with it we curse men, who have
> been made in the similitude of God. Out of
> the same mouth proceed blessing and cursing.
> My brethren, these things ought not to be so.
> Does a spring send forth fresh water and
> bitter from the same opening? Can a fig tree,
> my brethren, bear olives, or a grapevine bear
> figs? Thus no spring yields both salt water and
> fresh.
>
> —James 3:7-12

Every kind of beast, bird, reptile, and creature has been
tamed, but God said there is only one thing that cannot be
tamed—your tongue. No man can tame the tongue. It is an
unruly evil. It is full of deadly poison. It takes a move of God
to keep that tongue under subjection. It takes the power of
the Holy Spirit.

It sounds to me like the devil can stay *outside* because our
biggest issue is ourselves. We set hell on fire with our
tongues. We struggle because we seek to speak blessing and
cursing out of the same mouth. You cannot bless creation
over here and then point out the ugliness over there.
Blessing and cursing cannot flow from the same tongue.

The Scripture says "honor all people" (1 Peter 2:17). We don't have to agree with each other, or even like each other, but we are not to kill with the poison of our tongues. I am not supposed to degrade you, talk about you, minimize you, beat you up, or tell you how wrong you are. That is poison.

Spirit and Flesh Don't Mix

Many Christians seek to draw others into the Kingdom by preaching on sin and hell. They try to bring about repentance through condemnation. Romans 2:4 says, "Or do you despise the riches of His goodness, forbearance, and longsuffering, not knowing that the goodness of God leads you to repentance?"

Could that be why we are not having more souls saved— because we are trying to draw men to repentance with fear, intimidation, ugliness, and backstabbing? Could that be why people are not repenting? When you preach the goodness of God it draws people to repentance. When you preach hell, you are on your own. The Scripture says that "saviors" shall come up on Mount Zion to judge (Obadiah 1:21). What do saviors do? They deliver, set free, and talk about the goodness of God; because the goodness of God causes men to repent.

I do not know why we have come to a place where we are judging everybody and everything. We are all different, and we each have our own path set before us. There are different visions, different expectations. 1 Corinthians 12:17-19 says, "If the whole body were an eye, where would be the hearing?

If the whole were hearing, where would be the smelling? But now God has set the members, each one of them, in the body just as He pleased. And if they were all one member, where would the body be?" We need to embrace the unique qualities in each member in order to properly function as a whole body, lacking nothing.

Why are we judging someone else when we have a full-time job keeping ourselves in line? We need to grow up. We have to stop trying to mix spirit and flesh. We cannot whole-heartedly follow God and simultaneously talk about people behind their backs. We need to stop trying to follow the commandments in one place, while turning around to make fun of a brother or sister in another. Those things do not mix. Do not become hell to somebody. Some have hell in their own tongues, and bring it by the words of their mouth. You don't have to go to hell; hell will come to you!

After warning about the danger of the tongue, James continues:

> Who is wise and understanding among you? Let him show by good conduct that his works are done in the meekness of wisdom. But if you have bitter envy and self-seeking in your hearts, do not boast and lie against the truth. This wisdom does not descend from above, but is earthly, sensual, demonic. For where envy and self-seeking exist, confusion and *every* evil thing are there.
> —James 3:13-16 (emphasis added)

Keep your mouth off people. Keep your thoughts pure. You are not going to be perfect but are to strive towards perfection. Thoughts carry power; they are vibrations and imaginations. They have the capability to set on fire the course of hell. Beloved, watch your ideas, your thoughts, your mouths, and your hearts; watch your judgments and criticism. Do not allow bitter and sweet water to come out of the same temple; let there be sweetness only. Speak positively always. Even if somebody is doing something ugly, seek to see him or her through God's eyes.

You will discover that everybody has potential and purpose when you see them as God sees them. God knows that people who intentionally injure someone else are acting out of a deranged and altered mindset. They don't know God. They are victims of themselves, oblivious to the Truth. Imagine if instead of *reacting* to other people's sins, insults, or injuries, we were able to have the presence of mind to bring healing, restoration, and Truth to those people— ultimately changing their mindsets! How different the Church would look if instead of playing the victim, we realized that all of mankind is victim to itself. We can bring the restoration and freedom that comes through Jesus! What a calling we have to step into!

The Battle of Armageddon

It has been traditionally taught that the battle of Armageddon is a showdown between the army of God and the army of the Satan that will take place at the end of the age (Revelations 16). Most Christians believe it will be a physical battle between physical enemies in some geographically located place on earth, resolving once and for all the conflict between good and evil.

Where is the real battle of Armageddon? It lies between the two natures; between the lower nature and the higher nature; between what *you* want to do and what *Christ* wants to do through you; between your old man and your new man. Where is the battle of Armageddon? It is in your mind. You are not wrestling with flesh and blood; you are wrestling with what *you* want to do, with what *you* think, with what grandma said, and what granddaddy said. It is not flesh and blood, but doctrines, principles, conditions, thoughts, lies, and fairytales.

The valley it takes place in, is the cleft—or the breach—between the right side and the left side of your brain, which represent the spirit and the soul; the old man and the new man. That cleft is the valley of decision. When that breach is repaired, flesh will be swallowed up by spirit, mortality will put on immortality, corruption shall put on incorruption, and we will be changed—that very moment! When the eye sees correctly and is full of light, our restored vision will affect our whole body. Just as the tongue has the power to steer us towards hell, when we see with enlightened eyes, we manifest heaven.

Recognizing the Battle

James asks, "Where do wars and fights come from among you? Do they not come from your desires for pleasure that war in your members?" (James 4:1). We often want to have our own way—no matter what it costs or whom it hurts. Where do fights come from? Your desire to be above God, your desire to be your own God, your tendency to say "God I know you want me to control my mouth, but I am not going to. God I know you want me to sow, but I am not going to. God I know you want me to pray, but I am not going to."

We follow our own passions to the detriment of our souls. We become blinded by our desire, oblivious to the pain we cause. Essentially, we tell God, "I want this and I don't care how it happens or who gets hurt in the process. I want this man or woman, and I don't care if I have to break up a marriage or break up a family in order to have him or her. I will get what I want." That is a war in your members. Will you abide by God's will or your own lusts? What exactly are your motives? That is the true Battle of Armageddon.

Jesus told Peter, "Most assuredly, I say to you, when you were younger, you girded yourself and walked where you wished; but when you are old, you will stretch out your hands, and another will gird you and carry you where you do not wish" (John 21:18).

When you are young you come, go, and do as you please. But when you mature, you put away childish things. Then the Holy Ghost will lead you and take you to where you do not want to go. That is a picture of our life in God; when we are young we want our own way, but then we mature and are led by the Holy Ghost. We begin to do what God calls us to do. We start listening to the new man. We grow up! We do not always get to go our own way!

You cannot have friendship with the world while following God. There is a system in which the world operates. The world is not a physical place. Instead it is a way of thinking outside the wisdom of God. It is a way of doing things. You cannot come into agreement with that system. That is why the kingdoms of this world must become the Kingdom of our Lord and Christ (Revelation 11:15). The world's system is decreasing and the Kingdom of God is increasing. You must stay in the system called the Kingdom. The Kingdom is higher. It is impossible to abide in two opposing systems. Developing a friendship with the systems of the world isn't compatible with the way of the Kingdom. Whoever wants to be a friend of the world makes himself an enemy before God (James 4:4).

The true battle lies within. We must overcome our own selfish desires. We must walk by the Spirit and let the new man conquer the old man. Our wrestling match is against ourselves, not against the devil. He will not have an entry way into your life if you stop making him a bed and telling him to come in and lay down. The plane can't land where there is no runway! Don't give Satan a runway. Don't give him a chance to come into agreement with the old man. Don't give him power that is not due him. Do not use the devil as a crutch to continue to do what you want to do. Don't blame your own works of the flesh on the devil. We must learn to discern the difference between the devil and our own flesh. Chapter 4 will give us some insight in this.

Chapter 4
Works of the Flesh

While I am ministering, I often tell the story about my friend who called me one day, asking for prayer. She said the devil got in her washing machine and it stopped working. I chuckled and replied, "Honey, it's not the devil in your washing machine. Your machine is just old, its just time for a new one!" For so many people, the devil is everywhere – he's in the bush, he rides with them in their car, and he waits on them to show up at work or school. I believe much of this concern comes from one's own imagination, born out of a consciousness that needs to be elevated to a higher realm.

Beyond Warfare

Walking in the anointing of God is supposed to feel natural to us. Once that new man is raised up, miracles will overflow from our lives. We will begin to do the greater works that Jesus was talking about (John 14:12). We will bring life to those around us. It should be *unnatural* for anything else to flow from us. Bitter water and sweet water don't come from the same source; an apple tree doesn't produce figs. Likewise, when Christ is living in us it should be *natural* to operate in accordance with the Spirit. The Spirit of God flows through us, blesses us, and encourages us.

Most of the time, we are hindered because we give the devil too much credit. We have already observed that he started out in Genesis as a serpent, and by the time we get to Revelation, he becomes an enormous dragon reaching the heavens (Revelation 12). We give Satan power by focusing on him. We have loosed him into the world; we have exalted him into the heavens. And not only have we loosed him, but we have fed him with our mouth and with our tongue. The power of life and death is in the tongue (Proverbs 18:21). We have fed him so much life with our voice that he has now become a great dragon that can only be dealt with by sons of God.

We need a new approach to warfare. Centering our attention on the devil doesn't work. We blame the devil for things that we should be taking responsibility for ourselves! Instead of coming before God in humility and repentance, we rebuke the devil. We have already exhausted this tactic! The results are far from satisfactory—the more we talk, the more we feed the devil and cause his influence to grow.

James tells us: "Therefore submit to God. Resist the devil and he will flee from you" (James 4:7). This is where effective warfare is found. That word *flee* means to *run as in terror.*

The devil will take flight in fear—provided that we submit to God. No rebuke needed.

So what does it mean to submit to God? Submission is a position of the heart, a perspective, a way of thinking. It comes from a transformed mind and manifests in thought, motive, and word. In order to fully submit to God, we have to operate with the mind of Christ. Paul exhorts us: "Let this mind be in you which was also in Christ Jesus..." (Philippians 2:5).

Going beyond warfare means that we submit to God, recognize and resist the devil, and he flees in terror from us. The futile warfare that we are currently engaging in can be corrected through prayer, fasting, and setting our vision and minds on God. It's a genuine plea for the renewal of Jesus in our own thinking—not an outburst of rebuke towards the devil.

We don't need another revelation. We need to embrace what God has already revealed to us, the work He is already performing. Old things are passing away and all things are becoming new (2 Corinthians 5:17). John the Baptist said, "He must increase, but I must decrease" (John 3:30). You and God can't both fit in the same place together. He is a large God. In fact, He will increase regardless of what you do, because He is making all things new. You will decrease, whether you want to or not.

I knew this to be true in my own life when God stepped in to make some changes. Personally, I would have been content to live a quiet, simple life in the country teaching my Sunday school class. That worked for a while. But when God began to increase in my life, invitations to teach the Word began to pour in from all over the world. Though I was content to remain where I was, I understood that the beginning era of my life and ministry had to decrease in order to make room for the future that God had planned for me. I was terrified. The choice was not my own, because God was in charge. I realize now that I had no reason to fear. We might as well save ourselves the struggle by joining Him in His redemptive work and positioning ourselves to decrease. In the end, someone has to give—and it won't be God!

We must come to a place of maturity and stop blaming the devil. Paul describes the process of growing up: "When I was a child, I spoke as a child, I understood as a child, I thought as a child; but when I became a man, I put away childish things" (1 Corinthians 13:11). If we are to grow up into Him, we must put away childish things and take responsibility for ourselves. When we quit blaming everything on the devil he loses his power. His influence diminishes. He is reduced to fleeing in terror. Owning up to our own wrongs, repenting, and continuing in submission to God can allow us to walk in continual freedom.

Beyond the Law

We often live, think, and operate as if we have to do something to merit God's love and favor. We try to earn God's healing, or pray the right words in the right fashion to get the desired result. Many have been led to believe that the laws of the Bible are restricting and designed to work against them. On the contrary, the laws of the Bible are for us, not against us. There aren't many things that God requires of us. Scripture tells us, "For all the law is fulfilled in one word, even in this: 'You shall love your neighbor as yourself'" (Galatians 5:14). God says all of His law is fulfilled when you love your neighbor. There is no need to get hung up on the details. Love God, and love creation!

Hebrews tells us:

> For on the one hand there is an annulling of the former commandment because of its weakness and unprofitableness, for the law made nothing perfect; on the other hand, there is the bringing in of a better hope, through which we draw near to God.
>
> —Hebrews 7:18-19

You can act right, do right, speak right, sing right, and baptize right; but the law makes nothing perfect. The law of Moses did not work. It wasn't effective in bringing men closer to God. We had to come face to face with our own depravity and need for a Savior. Men are not capable of externally following the law. We cannot work our way to perfection. It must come from the inside out.

God was not satisfied with the law. The law was temporary. The blood of bulls and goats could not change the hearts of men. If we are going back to that law, back to Jerusalem, back to the temple made by human hands—then we are heading in the wrong direction! Paul explains:

> Not that I have already attained, or am already perfected; but I press on, that I may lay hold of that for which Christ Jesus has also laid hold of me. Brethren, I do not count myself to have apprehended; but one thing I do, *forgetting those things which are behind and reaching forward to those things which are ahead*, I press toward the goal for the prize of the upward call of God in Christ Jesus.
> —Philippians 3:12-14 (emphasis added)

We are not going back to sacrificing bulls and goats. We are not going back to God dwelling in a temple made with human hands—that's going backwards! We are to view the past as examples and look ahead. God is taking us from the works of the flesh into the realm of the Spirit.

Judgment under the law has been completed through Christ. It already happened. All of us were pronounced guilty. We inherited death through Adam, but have now been raised to life through Christ (1 Corinthians 15:22). We now live according to the Spirit; and the Scripture tells us that if you "...are led by the Spirit, you are not under the law" (Galatians 5:18).

The law centers on actions, deeds, and on the things we do. God wants to take us to a higher place. He wants us to operate in Spirit—but you can't work your way to this place through the flesh. We are going beyond warfare into a place called mastery. God has fulfilled the former law; we are moving into the reality of the eternity of the Spirit. Paul tells us that when we walk in the Spirit, we do not fulfill the lusts of the flesh (Galatians 5:16).

The Lusts of the Flesh

Galatians 5 gives us a comprehensive list of the works of the flesh. These things, therefore, do not proceed from the devil:

> Now the works of the flesh are evident, which are: adultery, fornication, uncleanness, lewdness, idolatry, sorcery, hatred, contentions, jealousies, outbursts of wrath, selfish ambitions, dissensions, heresies, envy, murders, drunkenness, revelries, and the like; of which I tell you beforehand, just as I also told you in time past, that those who practice such things will not inherit the kingdom of God.
> —Galatians 5:19-21

When I read this passage I was amazed to realize that many of the things that we've been rebuking outside ourselves as the devil are not the devil at all; they're our flesh. We've been binding spirits, performing exorcisms, and tarrying at the altar over these things that we should have been rebuking within ourselves. This passage leaves us without excuse. In fact, to me, it is a pretty exhaustive list of what *is not* the devil. After reading this, it is clear that we cannot continue to blame the devil for any of these things.

All forms of sexual immorality or impurity come from the flesh. Adultery, fornication, uncleanness, and lewdness all proceed from the mind of man. The devil is not after you, trying to tempt you—you are simply giving in to your own desires, listening to your old nature.

Putting anything above God—any form of idolatry—comes from your own heart and must not be attributed to the devil.

Even sorcery is a result of the sinful mind of man, and does not proceed from the devil. If we live in accordance with the Spirit, we don't have to worry about any form of witchcraft or sorcery—because it proceeds from the flesh and only works in the flesh. Spirit and flesh don't mix!

When you hurt, insult, or injure another person because of hatred, contention, jealousy, anger, self-centeredness, dissension, envy, or any other disagreement—it comes from your own tendencies, not those of the devil! You will only be able to move past these things when you recognize their true source.

Murder—you may say, "I thought surely the devil was a murderer." Yes he is, but the Scripture says that when God deals with murderous tendencies in *you*, it's a work of the flesh. It comes from within.

At the end of the list we come to drunkenness and revelries—the luxuries of the world. You may think the devil is trying to tempt you to return to your old life, to join in the carelessness of the world. On the contrary, your own mind, your own flesh—your old nature—is the one attempting to take control, not the devil. The battle lies with*in*, not with*out!*

As long as we continue to blame the devil, we avoid having to change, repent, or grow up. God is calling us to grow up, mature, ask for forgiveness, and repent! Quit worrying about the devil on the outside and start taking care of the devil within—that old man of sin, that carnal man who only wants his own way. When we listen to the old man, the devil doesn't even have to show up. If you are already engaging in gossip, cruelty toward others, or jealousy—the devil is probably nowhere in sight! You are doing his job wonderfully, all by yourself! You are already living according to the flesh, so he has no need to interfere.

After Paul warns us about the works of the flesh, he says, "I also told you in time past, that those who practice such things will not inherit the kingdom of God" (Galatians 5:21). Paul doesn't say you won't go to heaven; he doesn't say you won't see the Kingdom; he doesn't say you won't enter in— but you will not inherit the power of the Kingdom unless you put away childish things, grow up, and walk in the Spirit.

To inherit the Kingdom means to be made a ruler and have dominion over the universe as we know it. The world in all its fullness belongs to the Lord (Psalm 24:1); the authority to rule it and inherit it comes from His hand. You can't rule the universe and inherit the Kingdom with jealousy; you can't inherit the Kingdom while backstabbing, being mean and ornery, or speaking death. You may be permitted to *see* the Kingdom, and even enter in, and God will work with you—but you will never *inherit* the power, authority, and dominion of God's Kingdom. Let us live by the Spirit so that we may inherit the Kingdom!

You Reap What You Sow

There is a principle in the Scripture of sowing and reaping. It is possible that some of the undesirable things that occur in your life happen because of this principle; sometimes you are reaping as a result of sowing contrary to the Spirit. Paul tells us in Galatians:

> Do not be deceived, God is not mocked; for whatever a man sows, that he will also reap. For he who sows to his flesh will of the flesh reap corruption, but he who sows to the Spirit will of the Spirit reap everlasting life.
> —Galatians 6:7-8

If you do not like the results you see, consider this: maybe the devil is not acting up—perhaps you are simply reaping flesh over things you haven't taken responsibility for. Whatever a man sows, that he will also reap (Galatians 6:7). We have sown into the flesh and we reap corruption. We are guilty of being mean, ornery, and backbiting. We've been hateful, and called it the devil. We mock God because we refuse to grow up. We pass over and judge the unbeliever.

We miss out on inheriting the whole kingdom. We forget that whatever we bind on earth is bound in heaven. We fall short of dying to ourselves and becoming a visible manifestation of an invisible God. Don't be deceived, because God is not mocked.

If you sow into the flesh, you will reap corruption—and it will not be from the devil. Flesh is flesh and the devil is the devil. Don't confuse them! It's the impure heart, mixed motives, and judgmental thinking of the flesh that we experience consequences from. Could it be that we are shifting blame to the devil when in reality we're simply reaping what we've sown?

God calls us to be transformed by the renewing of our minds (Romans 12:2). As long as you've got it in your mind to blame others, you'll never be transformed. As long as you think the fight is going on out there and you overlook the battle in your own heart, you will be hindered. Deal with the fight that's going on in your own heart and mind. Deal with your own selfish motives! We need to recognize and own up to the flesh within ourselves, so that we can move past it.

Sow into the Spirit

How much could God move if every one of us took responsibility for our flesh, resisted the devil, and sent him fleeing? What could God do if we quit sowing into the flesh? We have a continual harvest of corruption coming into the body of Christ, and we've called it the devil. God calls us to modify and bring into correction the deeds of our flesh. Paul tells us about the law of sin that works in our members. He says:

> For I know that in me (that is, in my flesh) nothing good dwells; for to will is present with me, but how to perform what is good I do not find. For the good that I will to do, I do not do; but the evil I will not to do, that I practice.
>
> —Romans 7:18-19

As long as you are in the flesh, you are going to have to keep check on your flesh. Be mindful of your own attitude, your own intentions, your own motives, and your own words. "First remove the plank from your own eye, and then you will see clearly to remove the speck from your brother's eye" (Matthew 7:5). I offer these personal words of wisdom: "Physician, heal thyself!"

Our flesh allows us to stay touchable to creation—because if there was no flesh to deal with, we might start to look down on others too easily. If you didn't deal with your own flesh, you might condemn and judge somebody else over the very thing that you do yourself. If you didn't live in this flesh every day, you could not be touched with the infirmities of people. The flesh is not a curse—it's going to be restored and renewed. We need to use the flesh to our advantage, since we are stuck with it anyway. The flesh should bring you to a place of mercy and compassion.

Paul tells us "Brethren, if a man is overtaken in any trespass, you who are spiritual restore such a one in a spirit of gentleness, considering yourself lest you also be tempted" (Galatians 6:1). We are to restore those who fall with gentleness—because we are liable to fall into the same trap. Each of us lives with this flesh. The flesh isn't an excuse to sin, but rather it points us toward a higher way to live. If we plant love, compassion, gentleness, and mercy, guess what you will reap? You got it! You will reap love, compassion, gentleness, and mercy.

God is love, and we know that perfect love casts out all fear (1 John 4:18). When the Church leans toward hatred and judgment towards others, it does not truly reflect God. It will reap a harvest of fear, torment, and judgment. When we judge others harshly, we often judge ourselves harshly—and live with guilt and condemnation as a result.

God is calling His people to a *higher* place! The Church must begin to sow unto the Spirit! When you cut other people slack, you also cut yourself some slack. When we sow goodness, kindness, gentleness, and mercy, that's exactly what we will receive! Sowing unto the Spirit will bring no loathing or self-condemnation. God never intended for you to have a list of rules and regulations that are impossible to bear. God meant for you to be in the flesh, grow up, and mature. Flesh must decrease, Spirit will increase, and you will begin to put on that incorruptible man, walking in love.

Let's identify flesh with flesh. Let's put the devil back in his place. Let's ask for the Spirit of wisdom and understanding that brings maturity. Children blame others for their own mistakes; grown men take responsibility. Let us put away childish things and become true sons of God. Let's recognize the works of our own flesh, so that we can move past them.

When we walk in the Spirit we become a visible manifestation of the invisible God. When we begin to mature, the devil decreases—and runs when he sees us coming! When we allow God to deal with us, we allow Him to increase more and more in our lives. We will begin to walk in the miraculous, naturally. Our shadows will heal. We will stop storms in their tracks. As flesh decreases and Christ increases, people will be healed by coming into our presence. We will shift the atmosphere wherever our feet tread. Broken bones and weakened joints will be restored. But in order to move in this miraculous realm, we must first grow up!

God wants His people to move into this realm of mastery, but we must be prepared. We must move beyond warfare with the devil, beyond the law, and beyond the flesh. We must embrace son-ship and inherit the whole Kingdom. We will then be given the authority to rule and have dominion. God is calling us to serve in His royal priesthood—the Melchizedek Priesthood, which is explored in the next chapter.

Chapter 5
The Melchizedek Priesthood

Thirty years ago, I began teaching what I believed was a groundbreaking truth that had been hidden in the Scripture—The Order of Melchizedek. I realized that the body of Christ at large wasn't quite ready for the depth of revelation I was sharing, so I was led to "seal my books" for a time. In recent years I have been again ministering on this "new priesthood"—not new to God, but new to us.

I believe we, as Abraham's seed, are about to be interrupted by a priesthood we have not seen for generations. The Melchizedek Priesthood will minister after the power and the source of an endless life. All of creation is groaning, waiting for the manifestation—or the placement—of the sons of God. These sons will become that priesthood called Melchizedek.

Manifesting the Father

We have seen the *sheep*—those who are satisfied with green pastures, content to follow the crowd. They have no desire to search deeper for the things of God, but remain satisfied with earthly pleasures. We have seen the *children*—those who enter into the house of God, but remain immature in understanding. We have seen the *bride*—those who are fixed on the wedding and union with Christ, but remain focused only on His return. And we have seen the *wife*—those who take care of other children in the house, and invest in their growth and maturity. She can legally use the name of God, as a legal partner in a marriage relationship. But we have not yet seen the *sons!*

The Church has grown progressively, but has not reached her final destination. We have yet to see the fullness of God expressed through a people. God has heard a cry He is about to answer: "show us the Father, and it is sufficient for us" (John 14:8).

Creation is not satisfied; it rages because the only thing that will satisfy it is seeing the Father in all His glory. We have seen doctrines, traditions, and religions. But this generation—this priesthood—will decree and declare the Father, and will be equipped to manifest the Father as sons. When we begin to express the Father as sons (mature ones), creation will enter into a healing that will be worldwide and move beyond the Church. It will spill over the church walls and bring lost children to the Father. The anointing of Melchizedek is to do the greater things Jesus talked about.

The anointing of the Melchizedek Priesthood is a high place in God called to minister to all of creation. Melchizedek is called to all nations, not just to the Church.

Tithes

Genesis 14 talks about Abraham's meeting with Melchizedek:

> Then Melchizedek king of Salem brought out bread and wine; he was the priest of God Most High. And he blessed him and said:
>
> "Blessed be Abram of God Most High,
> Possessor of heaven and earth;
> And blessed be God Most High,
> Who has delivered your enemies into your hand."
>
> And he gave him a tithe of all.
>   —Genesis 14:18-20

The practice of tithing is giving 10% of your entire livelihood. Tithes may include money or finances, but are certainly not limited to this area. Our tithes dictate whom we honor. Our priorities are revealed by examining who or what we tithe to: "No servant can serve two masters; for either he will hate the one and love the other, or else he will be loyal to the one and despise the other. You cannot serve God and mammon (Luke 16:13)." When we put personal wealth above our relationship with God, money becomes our master. But when we remain faithful in tithing to God above all else, He is our master.

We tend to get confused about the tithes. Some people in the Church abide by it, while others don't. Not only is the tithe legal, but it was established *before* the Levitical Priesthood. We gather from the Genesis passage that Abraham paid Melchizedek a tithe, even before Levi was born; the Levites had already paid tithe to a higher Priesthood while they were still unformed in Abraham's loins.

Under Levitical law, the priest took tithes from Israel. On the contrary, Abraham freely gave his tithe to Melchizedek. The tithes in the Levitical Priesthood were mandatory; but the tithes in the Melchizedek Priesthood are voluntary. Creation freely gives to the new Priesthood, honoring God above all else and releasing His blessings. When we give honor to God and show Him precedence, He blesses us. The Melchizedek Priesthood receives tithes, which release the blessings of God to creation. The tithe is not a law; it is a revelation of whom you honor. The tithe dictates who your master is.

If you are Abraham's seed—which you are—and heirs according to the promise, you were in Abraham when he tithed to Melchizedek. Abraham essentially tithed a people. Hebrews 7:9-10 explains: "Even Levi, who receives tithes, paid tithes through Abraham, so to speak, for he was still in the loins of his father when Melchizedek met him."

There is a place in God where you are already His, chosen in Him before the foundation of the world. Before He formed you in your mother's womb, He knew you, and had oneness with you. There is a place in God where you are secure. You were given to God in the loins of Abraham before you were even a thought in your daddy's mind. God has known His true sons before the foundation. We are His firstfruit; we are His tithe. We can run, slip, slide, peep, and hide—but at the end of the day, we will serve in the Priesthood.

Some people have the liberty to make their own choices; but there are some of us that have been marked by God before the foundation of the world, chosen in Him. I know this statement is in stark contrast to what many have been taught about free will; but I am suggesting that some of us have very few choices. If you could talk to Jonah, I imagine that he would tell you about free will. When God told him to go to Nineveh, he fought God to the extent that he chose a different destination, only to eventually end up in Nineveh after all. If you could talk to the Virgin Mary, she would tell you about God's sovereign choice. When the angel told her that she would have a son, she was troubled and confused. She said, "How can this be, since I do not know a man?" (Luke 1:34). She didn't have a choice. We are the ones creation is groaning for. We are the Priesthood that has been chosen to satisfy that groan by manifesting the Father.

Firstfruits

The Melchizedek Priesthood was ordained before the foundation. Maybe you feel its call. Are there places where you don't fit? Are you hungry for more than dead letters on the page? Do you desire to know God deeper, above all else? You may feel out of place as a *firstfruit* offered to God.

Israel was required to give firstfruits to God—the first ripened fruits of their harvest, the best fruits of the season. To give a firstfruit offering is an act of faith in expectation that the remainder of the harvest will be abundant. It is giving an offering from the harvest you expect to come, *before* it comes. What faith! Firstfruits can be distinguished from a generic tithe in that they are not simply a percentage of your earnings, but the best from what is yet to come.

Abraham tithed a people, a firstfruit that would look like they were out of place, because they bloomed early. They were ahead of their time. They were set apart from the rest of creation. They would know God in a way that other people may not even care to know Him.

The firstfruits blossom earlier than the rest of the harvest. The firstfruits yield fruit before the rest of the vine. It may seem like you are in the wrong place at the wrong time; but on the contrary, you have been born into this age for a very specific reason. You are a firstfruits harvest. The firstfruits are the sweetest of the fruit. They are the source of seeds to plant for the next season. They ripen first and show the Father the potential for rest of the harvest.

Even if you feel out of season, or out of time, you can find fulfillment in being the sweetest and most anointed firstfruit. You can live out a higher calling, unaffected by the cares of the world. Your situation doesn't shape you. You don't draw meaning from the things that go on around you. You *bring* meaning to the world and offer restoration to those who are cut off and suffering (Isaiah 61).

Communion

You are firstfruits. You have ripened early because you have been given communion. At some point, your life was interrupted and quickened. Melchizedek interrupted Abraham's life with communion. Immediately after Abraham took communion from Melchizedek, things in his life began to quicken.

After the sharing of the bread and wine, Abraham fathered Isaac at 100 years old (Genesis 21:5). Sarah delivered a baby at over 90 years old (Genesis 17:17). Even though Sarah wasn't present during the communion, she was affected. Even though Levi wasn't yet born, he was affected. We are also, as Abraham's seed, affected by the communion. Even though we weren't physically present with Abraham, we were still *in* Abraham. When you receive communion from Melchizedek, it is a timeless and generational communion.

During Melchizedek's meeting with Abraham, communion had not yet been established. Jesus had not yet come. The Levitical Priesthood was not yet in existence. The elements present in the bread and wine come out of the belly of a Priesthood that ministers life—endless life. Abraham had to be a partaker in the anointing even before the anointing was established. The anointing is the only thing that quickens mortal flesh (Romans 8:11); and with Abraham there had to be a quickening of the flesh when the Scripture calls him "as good as dead" (Hebrews 11:12; Romans 4:19).

What power could accomplish such things? What brings life from death? What alters the course of a life? Communion from the belly of a true priest after the order of Melchizedek. Halleluiah!

In Genesis 14:18, the Scripture states that Melchizedek "brought forth bread and wine..." (King James Version). That word "brought forth" has the same thought as the word used when the Virgin Mary "brought forth" Jesus from her womb (Luke 2:7). Melchizedek brings forth communion from the power and the source of endless life. Melchizedek brought forth from his belly, just like the Virgin Mary brought forth from her belly. Melchizedek is the author and the finisher of communion. Melchizedek is the Priesthood that God established from before the foundation of the world to minister to all of creation.

The Circumcision

What happens to Abraham once he takes communion from Melchizedek? What happens to you once you take communion from the Melchizedek Priesthood? Several things begin to happen. One of the first things Abraham did was to go back to his house and circumcise everything.

Circumcision means to cut off excess flesh in order to be able to reproduce better. I believe the whole Church is about to be circumcised; but this is a different kind of circumcision. The first circumcision was of the body; the coming circumcision will be of the mind and the heart. This circumcision will be examined further in the next chapter.

Who is Melchizedek?

What more does the Scripture say about Melchizedek? The Scripture says that Melchizedek was the King of Salem, meaning King of Peace (Hebrews 7:2). Melchizedek was not from a geographically located place—Melchizedek was priest over a realm. Salem represents the Garden, that whole realm of dominion that man lost. Melchizedek fed that dominion back into Abraham. Abraham did not eat from the wrong tree; he chose the Tree of Life. The communion he shared with Melchizedek nourished the seed that was in Abraham's loins; it was established as Abraham ate. The tithe was given and the firstfruits were selected. The firstfruits guarantee the rest of the harvest by faith. We are included in that harvest to receive the inheritance.

Melchizedek is the King of Peace. Peace is not something that is tangible; it is a realm. I believe there is only one person Melchizedek could be. Melchizedek was not birthed in the flesh; he had neither mother nor father, neither beginning nor end (Hebrews 7:3). There was only one other man that did not come through a womb in the whole Scripture—the first Adam. I believe Melchizedek is *you*, returning to your fullness in God, giving communion to all of creation. Melchizedek is the new man. Creation is groaning for the manifestation of the true sons of God—those who serve in the Melchizedek Priesthood.

The Seal of God

Revelation 7:1-2 says, "After these things I saw four angels standing at the four corners of the earth, holding the four winds of the earth, that the wind should not blow on the earth, on the sea, or on any tree. Then I saw another angel ascending from the east, having the seal of the living God."

East always represents the dawning of a new day. East also represents Eden; because Eden, which is the realm we are waking up to, was planted eastward (Genesis 2:8). Remember, Jesus said His coming would be revealed from the east to the west (Matthew 24:27). He will reveal Himself as the Alpha and Omega; the Beginning and the End; the First and the Last—from Eden to the Kingdom. Christ will manifest himself anew *within* a people, to all of creation.

Revelation 8:1 says, "When He opened the seventh seal, there was silence in heaven for about half an hour." Why is there a silence? There is a silence because God's work is finished in you. Creation is on its way to the graveyard—one big funeral procession. But just as Jesus did, you will interrupt the funeral procession and resurrect what was dead. Creation will taste of life, endless life, life in its fullness— through you!

Scripture tells us of two marks: the mark of God and the mark of the beast (Revelation 7:3; Revelation 13:16-17). In the King James Version, both marks are said to be sealed "in" the forehead. It does not say "on" the forehead, because the marks represent a way of thinking. They are a way of

82

understanding, a way of knowledge. The mark of the beast is already here. Paul talked about the many antichrists of his day (1 John 2:18). As mentioned in Chapter 1, "anti" doesn't mean *against*, it means *instead of*. We worship many things instead of God. That is the mark of the beast. You can tell if someone has the mark of the beast by the way they think. It is a mindset that drives them to operate in accordance with the world and their carnal desires.

The mark of God, on other hand, is having His name written in your forehead. It means having His nature walked out in your thinking. Be comfortable with the fact that you don't fit in. We are supposed to see things differently than the world sees them. We are supposed to think with the transformed mind of Christ. If you don't see differently than the world does, that indicates a very limited vision that needs to be elevated.

We are set apart as the firstfruits. The firstfruits ripen early, and are a foretaste of the coming harvest. You are God's evidence and proof that there is about to be a new move in the earth. It will bring forth a priesthood—the Melchizedek Priesthood—that is going to release the power and the source of endless life to a hurting creation. It is the ultimate communion. And it is being brought forth from you!

Chapter 6
The God of Your Ishmaels

Looking back over my life, there are things I would do differently, given the opportunity. Like most people, I wish I could change some of my past behaviors, thoughts, and actions. I am convinced, however, that we are too hard on ourselves when it comes to the "would haves, could haves, or should haves" of our past. Each day, I believe that God requires us to make the best decisions possible with the information, experience, and resources that we have available to us. Outside of this, He is responsible for making sense of our lives while managing the details that make it up.

What is an "Ishmael?"

God made a covenant with Abraham, and promised him many offspring (Genesis 15:5). Yet Abraham and his wife Sarah became advanced in years, and still they had no offspring. Instead of waiting on God, they impatiently decided to take action on their own. Sarah told Abraham to sleep with her maiden Hagar, in order to bear him a child and continue his line. Hagar was a stand-in. Abraham agreed, and soon Hagar had conceived a child. After Hagar became pregnant, tensions between Sarah and Hagar ran high. Eventually Sarah got so jealous that she kicked Hagar out of the household and Hagar fled into the wilderness to hide. There, an angel of the Lord met her and prophesied to her of Ishmael's birth. Hagar returned to Sarah in submission, and later gave birth to Ishmael (Genesis 16).

Even though Sarah and Abraham had acted on their own to conceive Ishmael, God still delivered on His promise. They miraculously conceived and bore Isaac in their old age, who became heir to all that God had promised Abraham (Genesis 21:2). But what about Ishmael?

Ishmael is what some people would call a mistake, a thing of the flesh. Ishmael is the name people give for the things you did before you were in your right mind. But did you know that God will circumcise even your "Ishmaels" and use them in the Kingdom? God is also the God of Ishmaels. He is going to take your low times, your mistakes, and your desires of the flesh and circumcise them, cut the flesh off, and then produce fruit from them.

I believe that everything you have been through in your life has had the handprint of God on it. There is a divine plan for your life. All the trials that you have been through have shaped you to be the person you are today.

God said, "I form the light and create darkness..." (Isaiah 45:7). John tells us "All things were made through Him, and without Him nothing was made that was made" (John 1:3). Again, the Lord says, "For I know the thoughts that I think toward you, says the Lord, thoughts of peace and not of evil, to give you a future and a hope" (Jeremiah 29:11). Everything you walk through is bringing you to a place of maturity so that you know how to walk and operate in the Kingdom.

None of us was born perfect. We may have done some stupid things in the past; but there is nothing that is beyond God's redemption. He continues to circumcise our mistakes and bring forth good from evil. He will restore to you the years that the locust has eaten (Joel 2:25). He will make up for lost time.

Sometimes people are ashamed to share their testimonies. They feel embarrassed and guilty of the things that happened while they were still dead in their sins. Yet God redeems *every part* of our lives. Instead of lingering on the evil in the past, thank God for the work He has done and continues to do in you! Thank God that He is able to take fallen man and restore him. Be grateful that we are able to walk in the fullness of God with a vision to reach out to the lowest of the low. God will let nothing go to waste.

Abraham had an Ishmael that had to be dealt with. Genesis 21 continues his story. As Ishmael and Isaac grew, Ishmael's presence began to aggravate Sarah (Genesis 21:10). Ishmael's mother did not help matters, but only made them worse. Sarah decided that she wanted them both to leave.

She wanted to be separated from them. God told Abraham to listen to what Sarah wanted. Ishmael and Hagar fled into the wilderness once again, where God Himself provided for them (Genesis 21:17-20). Ishmael lived in separation from the true heir, but he was still blessed by God.

Do you know there are things you have done that you need to be separated from? They may not be bad things; but they need to go, all the same.

God Uses Our Ishmaels

We tend to think of Ishmael as Abraham's mistake; but when Hagar left with Ishmael and put him under the bush to die, she cried out and God *Himself* spoke to Hagar (Genesis 21:17-18). We all have Ishmaels we have birthed, but have you ever considered that God wants to use those Ishmaels? God had a use for both Isaac, the promised child, *and* Ishmael. God promised Abraham, "And as for Ishmael, I have heard you. Behold, I have blessed him, and will make him fruitful, and will multiply him exceedingly. He shall beget twelve princes, and I will make him a great nation" (Genesis 17:20).

The Scripture tells us that at the time of Abraham's death, his sons Ishmael and Isaac buried him (Genesis 25:9). There is no mention of Abraham's other descendants, only Ishmael and Isaac. The place where he was buried is called Machpelah (Genesis 25:9), which in the Hebrew means "*double* [portion]." God used Abraham's Ishmael—his "mistake"—to doubly bless him! Ishmael was not a surprise to God, but part of His divine plan. Your own Ishmaels don't surprise God either!

Remember the story of Joseph in Genesis 37. He was the favorite of his father Jacob, whom he had given the beautiful coat of many colors. His brothers were jealous of him and threw him into a pit to die. Joseph would have died there had it not been for Abraham's "mistake"—the Ishmaelites. The Ishmaelites got Joseph out of the pit, saved his life, and took him to Egypt where he could fulfill his purpose (Genesis 37:28). Don't ever think that God can't use your "Ishmaels"!

Sometimes it takes an Ishmael to get to a promise. It took an Ishmael to get Abraham to the promise. Likewise, you have had to learn things along the way, before arriving at your destination. Learning can be painful. It took an Ishmael to give Abraham the wisdom to know what to do with Isaac when he came. If you have never dealt with an Ishmael, you will never know what to do with an Isaac. Letting go of Ishmael was a sacrifice—but God didn't forsake Ishmael. And then when God told him to sacrifice Isaac, Abraham knew from experience that all things would work together for good (Romans 8:28). God wastes nothing.

The Circumcision of Our Ishmaels

You need to know that you cannot do anything ugly enough or stupid enough for God not to use. If you will circumcise your Ishmael—by cutting off the flesh—*you will see God in it.* To circumcise a mistake means to cut the flesh away, and see God's purpose behind it. God has used *everything* in your life to shape you, teach you, and cause you to grow. After you cut the flesh from your mistake, lay it before the Lord, and learn from it, He will use it abundantly. God wastes nothing. Once it's circumcised, God can use it.

Abraham circumcised Ishmael. By the time I figured this out, I had a whole line of Ishmaels waiting to be circumcised. I told God it was going to take him awhile to deal with all the Ishmaels I still had attached to me. After I let Him circumcise some things that I had been through, I began to see His purpose take shape. It didn't always feel good, and it wasn't always easy, but the Lord works all things *for our good.* Romans 8:28-29 became very real to me. I let go of self-consciousness in ministry; I stopped trying to please man and worked to please God alone; I realized it was okay for people not to agree with me, and I didn't have to react by getting hurt or offended. I was no longer a slave to the opinion of man; instead I became a slave to the purpose of God. Cutting these things off gave me freedom. God was showing me who he had called me to be. He showed me purpose behind my Ishmaels.

Genesis 17:3-5 tells about Abraham's name change: "Then Abram fell on his face, and God talked with him, saying: 'As for Me, behold, My covenant is with you, and you shall be a father of many nations. No longer shall your name be called Abram, but your name shall be Abraham; for I have made you a father of many nations.'" After you circumcise your Ishmaels, God is going to give you a new identity.

Up until the day of circumcision, God had said to Abraham, "Lift your eyes now and look from the place where you are—northward, southward, eastward, and westward; for all the land which you see I give to you and your descendants forever" (Genesis 13:14b-15). After Abraham took communion from Melchizedek, God said: "Look now toward heaven..." (Genesis 15:5).

Melchizedek will stretch your vision to include not only the earth, but the heavens also. When you receive communion from Melchizedek, God will change your name—He will change your very nature, and you will be supernatural. When the new man receives life from the Holy Spirit, you will be forever changed. Once you allow Him to deal with the Ishmaels that are holding you back, your mind will be renewed. Then things will begin to fall into place, like puzzle pieces coming together.

Circumcising our Ishmaels involves repentance. Repentance is when we acknowledge mistakes in our lives, ask for forgiveness, and then turn from those ways. We realize that we were on a trajectory headed one direction, and then we turn around completely and head the other direction. Repentance is *not* stalling on the road and letting sin stop you dead in your tracks. We often come to the altar on Sunday morning to repent over hurts that happened 50 years ago. My mother Granny Matt says that when you do something stupid, or bring hurt to someone else, you should kneel at the foot of the cross and repent; but then get up and let somebody else take his or her turn! Move on. Don't hog the foot of the cross!

Some people have been lying at the cross for 20 years. We need to stop being so self-focused and preoccupied with our own lives. We need to stop letting sin get the last word and fix our eyes upon the One who has removed it from us!

Instead of carrying guilt and shame over past mistakes, give them to God, and allow Him to use them. God makes everything beautiful in its time (Ecclesiastes 3:11). Nothing takes Him by surprise. We cannot hold on to our problems and expect to keep growing in God. We need to circumcise them. Circumcision gives us a spiritual perspective. Circumcision helps us see the big picture. Circumcision helps us heal.

Death Influences Destiny

Going back even further than Abraham, we can understand how God shaped the lives of both Ishmael and Isaac. The short passage at the end of Genesis 11 indicates that Terah—Abraham's father—was called to the Promised Land. It states: "This is the genealogy of Terah: Terah begot Abram, Nahor, and Haran. Haran begot Lot. And Haran died before his father Terah in his native land, in Ur of the Chaldeans" (Genesis 11: 27-28). The passage continues in verse 31:

> And Terah took his son Abram and his grandson Lot, the son of Haran, and his daughter-in-law Sarai, his son Abram's wife, and they went out with them from Ur of the Chaldeans to go to the land of Canaan; and they came to Haran and dwelt there. So the

days of Terah were two hundred and five years, and Terah died in Haran.

—Genesis 11:31-32

We know that Terah's son Haran died in Ur, and that some time afterwards Terah continued to lead his family to the land of Canaan. However, we read that when they came to a place called Haran, they stayed there. Terah died in Haran. Terah could not move beyond the pain of his son's death, and chose to dwell in that place instead of stepping into the fullness of where God was calling him. What you do with death dictates how you will move in the fullness of God. Every person on the planet will encounter death at some point in life. We will all come across a situation where something doesn't go our way. What will you do when something, or someone, dies? You can either dwell on it, or you can move on and listen for what God has to say. What you do with that death dictates how great your destiny becomes.

What you do with what dies around you also dictates which god you serve. Terah ended up worshipping other gods at some point (Joshua 24:2). Even something as painful as loss can become an idol in our lives, and take the place of the very God who holds all things in His hands.

Terah was 70 years old when he had Abraham (Genesis 11:26). Abraham was about 100 years old when both Ishmael and Isaac had been born to him (Genesis 21:5). This means that Terah was 170 years old when his grandsons Ishmael and Isaac were both alive. Terah didn't die until he was 205 years old (Genesis 11:32). He still had plenty of years left to live during the time when Ishmael and Isaac were young men. Terah was still alive!

Tradition would have dictated that Abraham take his sons to their grandfather to be blessed. But God had other plans. God wanted a new covenant. God did not consider Terah alive. He interrupted the traditions of men and made a new covenant with Abraham, replacing Terah and putting Himself as Abraham's father. The Lord Himself blessed Abraham's sons, and they began to fulfill their purpose.

Terah's reaction to the death of his son hindered his destiny to walk in the fullness of God. Instead, Abraham was given a double inheritance through his own fleshly mistake, Ishmael. We can also see how King David, a man after God's heart, dealt with his own "Ishmael." David's fleshly mistake took form through the woman Bathsheba. 2 Samuel 11-12 details the whole story. David lusted after Bathsheba, and had her husband Uriah killed. With her husband out of the way, David married Bathsheba and a son was born to them. However the Lord was not pleased with David's behavior, and the child became ill and died (2 Samuel 12:18).

How did David respond to the death of his son? David had fasted and mourned when his son was ill, hoping that God would let him live. But after his death, the Scripture says, "David arose from the ground, washed and anointed himself, and changed his clothes; and he went into the house of the Lord and worshiped. Then he went to his own house; and when he requested, they set food before him, and he ate" (2 Samuel 12:20). David continued to worship and follow after

God. It wasn't long before Solomon—one of Israel's greatest kings—was born to David (2 Samuel 12:24).

What was the purpose of David having a dead child? If you don't know what to do with a dead child, you won't know what to do with a Solomon. David had special training in remaining faithful with that first death.

You don't know what to do with the anointing of God until you've had something die around you. God has a covenant with all of creation—He uses "life" to get you to where you're supposed to be. Even when our own fleshly mistakes result in tragedy, God uses them to serve a purpose. Don't underestimate the significance of even the most terrible Ishmaels! At the end of the day, whatever mistake you make, adversity you go through, or disappointment you experience, God is in control and has His handprint and purpose behind all of it.

Get Over It

A lot of people disagree about Ishmael and Isaac—but they both moved on! We must be about the Father's business. You have made mistakes in your life, no doubt. You have done some questionable things. You have hurt other people, and allowed other people to influence what you do. But God sees our repentant hearts. God is going to make something good from evil. He makes everything beautiful in its time (Ecclesiastes 3:11). No matter what junk you have been through in your life, God can make it beautiful. Even your Ishmaels have a purpose. God is that big! Have faith that He will keep you on track and finish the work He started in you (Philippians 1:6).

Things may not always *look* wonderful around us. Circumcision won't *feel* good. The situations we find ourselves in may not seem "good." But remember that the renewed mind doesn't make judgments based on outward appearances. Our senses don't discern good and evil. The eyes of faith are able to see God's purposes in everything.

God is a big enough God to keep you on track. We will look more at this Great Big God in the next chapter.

Chapter 7
Great Big God

I believe in a great big God and a real little devil. Many people believe there are devils everywhere. They choose to bring the devil with them in their minds wherever they go! In doing this, they make him bigger than he really is. There is only One who is present everywhere, who sees all things, who knows all things. He is the Alpha and the Omega, the First and the Last.

How big is your God? Is He a God that allows the devil to run rampant, killing anybody that he wants to? Is your God big enough to oversee not only your blessings, but your tribulations too? Or is He a God that is continuously working to clean up the devil's mess? To clean up Adam's mess? To clean up *your* mess?

Sovereign God

God asked Jonah to go to Nineveh to spread His word. Jonah promptly headed as far as he could in the opposite direction; he got on a ship bound for Tarshish (Jonah 1:3). Jonah thought he was getting away with disobeying God. What he didn't understand was that he was just taking the long route, and would in fact, end up in Nineveh as God desired.

You can go by way of a whale belly if you want to, but God will get you to where you are supposed to be—on time. He is a big enough God to intervene supernaturally. He will interrupt the normal digestive process of the whale in order to hold you in place. Sometimes God holds you in place until you come into your right mind.God knows the thoughts and intents of man's heart (Jeremiah 17:10). God knew that Adam was going to fall before he fell. The Lamb was slain before the foundation (1 Peter 1:20; Revelation 13:8). There may be times where you're in the dark, when you can't see the big picture, when God's redemptive plan is hidden from you. You only need to resolve one thing: *how big is your God?*

Colossians 1:16-17 states: "For by Him all things were created that are in heaven and that are on earth, visible and invisible, whether thrones or dominions or principalities or powers. All things were created through Him and for Him. And He is before all things, and in Him all things consist."

Again, John 1:3 says: "All things were made through Him, and without Him nothing was made that was made."

King David exclaims in Psalm 139:8:

If I ascend into heaven, You are there;
If I make my bed in hell, behold, You are there.

God encompasses all things. He does not stop at the gates of hell, as if that area was out of His jurisdiction. God is able to guide you through dark times, and walk with you even through your "hell seasons"—especially through your hell seasons! He is a great, big God!

Do we really know God? Do we live as though we worship the very Creator of the universe, the God who spoke all things into existence? Do we take it for granted that God holds all things in His hands?

Purposeful God

God created all things and God uses all things for His purposes (John 1:3). Throughout Moses' encounter with Pharaoh in the book of Exodus, we read of Pharaoh's hardened heart. God unleashed the ten plagues that brought destruction upon Egypt. Several times Pharaoh tried to release the Israelites, but God would harden his heart each time. God hardened Pharaoh's heart for a reason. He raised Pharaoh up to fulfill a specific role: "For the Scripture says to the Pharaoh, 'For this very purpose I have raised you up, that I may show My power in you, and that My name may be declared in all the earth'" (Romans 9:17).

Scripture tells us that Judas, too, fulfilled his purpose. Jesus said to his disciples: "Did I not choose you, the twelve, and one of you is a devil?" (John 6:70). Then later, during the last supper, Jesus revealed the one who would betray him. He says:

> "It is he to whom I shall give a piece of bread when I have dipped it." And having dipped the bread, He gave it to Judas Iscariot, the son of Simon. Now after the piece of bread, Satan entered him. Then Jesus said to him, "What you do, do quickly."
>
> —John 13:26-27

That word "quickly" refers to being *timely,* or *on schedule.* Jesus was encouraging Judas to fulfill his role on time, according to God's schedule. Judas was anointed to get Jesus to the cross on time. The timing of His crucifixion during Passover was crucial. If there had not been a Judas, the timing would have been off. Jesus had to go to the cross in God's perfect time.

Jesus had to be the perfect Lamb slain by God's own people in order to fulfill the law and make the sacrifice "legal." And so the Jews—the priesthood—offered him up. That is why Pontius Pilate washed his hands of responsibility (Matthew 27:24). God gave Pilate's wife a dream so he would not have anything to do with the sacrifice of Jesus (Matthew 27:19). The sacrifice would not have been acceptable if Jesus had been offered up by Pilate. Instead, the Sadducees and the Pharisees, who were the priesthood at that time, offered him up.

Do these insights wreck your theology? We may not always comprehend how God works. His ways are above ours. God has a purpose for everything that happens. No person is put in authority or dominion without the approval of God. What looks like evil at the time, only plays into God's hands and fulfills His purpose. God works all things for good. He is big enough to be in control.

As He did with the children of Israel, God may sometimes place a Pharaoh in your life to chase you to your destiny, so that you obtain your inheritance (Romans 9:17). God will put a Pharaoh in your life to chase you to a greater level of prosperity or health. God will put a Pharaoh in your life to keep you moving, even though you may be tired and looking to return to Egypt. No individual person is the focus of the story. It's not about you, or any other person. It's about God, and what He is accomplishing!

We have a free will, yes—but there is a line drawn in the sand. Jonah tried to make his own choice and ended up in the belly of the great fish (Jonah 1:17). Saul had a free will and he ended up on the ground, blind for three days (Acts 9:1-9). The children of Israel wanted to go back to Egypt, rather than die in the wilderness. They were grumbling, mumbling, and complaining—but when crossing the Red Sea was the only option available to them, they ran through on dry ground (Exodus 14). God's purpose prevailed. It is all about God. Your free will is going to take you a certain distance with God, but no more. You may not have chosen Him, but He has chosen *you*.

Let us pull the devil down and dethrone him. We have put him in the heavens when he was cursed to crawl on the dust of the ground. When you believe that God is a janitor, reduced to cleaning up after the devil—it affects how you believe, how you pray, and how you hear Him. It affects everything in your life. We know that faith comes by hearing, and hearing by the Word of God (Romans 10:17). Not the written word, but the Word that was made flesh and dwelt among us. Faith comes by hearing, and hearing by Jesus. Ask Jesus to give you the ability to hear with both ears, not just one. Ask Him for the ability to hear beyond the audible, to hear spiritually.

Wise God

Ephesians 3:8-9 says: "To me, who am less than the least of all the saints, this grace was given, that I should preach among the Gentiles the unsearchable riches of Christ, and to make all see what is the fellowship of the mystery, which from the beginning of the ages has been hidden in God who created all things through Jesus Christ..."

God's wisdom is manifold and all things work according to His order. We often try to use our own wisdom to explain God, instead of simply looking to Him. If something doesn't sit right with us, we force an answer on the issue instead of choosing to live with a lingering tension. We start making up fairytales to satisfy us, instead of taking the time to seek Him. The Bible says, "There is a way that seems right to a man, But its end is the way of death" (Proverbs 14:12; also 16:25). Real death is not the laying down of our natural bodies. Instead, according to the Scripture, to be carnally minded is death (Romans 8:6). The ways that seem right to our natural minds lean to the reasoning of the old nature.

The Scripture says:

> Trust in the Lord with all your heart
> And lean not on your own understanding;
> In all your ways acknowledge Him,
> And He shall direct your paths.
>
> —Proverbs 3:5-6

Do not rely on your own faulty thinking and reasoning. Don't try to resurrect the old man. Don't try to understand according to the flesh. Pull down the principles and doctrines; pull down the principalities and powers—the rulers of the darkness, thoughts and imaginations of this age, and the wickedness in high places. God is God all by Himself. Trust Him.

Transcendent God

It is hard for us to even comprehend operating outside of time and space, as we know it; but God is not limited by time. He created time, and put the seasons in their place. He said in the book of Peter, "But, beloved, do not forget this one thing, that with the Lord one day is as a thousand years, and a thousand years as one day" (2 Peter 3:8). When God talks about times and seasons he is not referencing them in a way we're accustomed to. He is not confined to days, hours, minutes, and seconds.

Throughout the Scripture, the prophets often used the words "time" and "season." When God talks of times and seasons, He is talking of any moment when the atmosphere is conducive for what He wills to do. The Scripture says that no one knows the day and hour of Christ's return at the consummation of the ages (Matthew 24:36). That is because God does not move in days and hours. He moves in seasons and times. The consummation of the ages will come in the season that the bride has made herself ready (Revelation 19:7).

Any time we try to get God to function according to our own agenda of a set time—like an hour or a year—His reply is very vague. Sometimes, we want to pull God into time and say, "God, do this tomorrow; do this by the fifteenth; I need an answer by next week." But God is not limited. He works outside of time. In eternity, time is a limitation. If we try to pull God into time, we limit our vision of Him. We only see a portion, not the fullness of Him as God.

God gave us time, as we know it, so that we can properly function in our day-to-day, earthly lives. We have seconds, minutes, hours, and days, so that we can get to where we are going and accomplish what we need to. But while living in time, God also anointed those who walk in Him to move in the realm of "timelessness." The Scripture tells us: "God is Spirit, and those who worship Him must worship in spirit and truth" (John 4:24). He has reserved for us the position of being in this flesh, but living and moving by the Spirit.

As we mentioned in previous chapters, flesh is trouble—it is the old man, the un-regenerated mind, and the obscured vision. But as the old man dies and the new man arises, God has reserved a place where we remain touchable to creation. God allows you to keep that bit of flesh to remind you how difficult it is to be of a fleshly nature. This is no license to sin. We know Jesus was human like us, and therefore also with a fleshly nature—yet without sin (Hebrews 4:15). He did not live according to His flesh. He walked by faith and not by sight. He walked in the Spirit.

Elijah also walked by the Spirit. Elijah commanded it not to rain according to his own word. He said, "As the Lord God of Israel lives, before whom I stand, there shall not be dew nor rain these years, *except at my word*" (1 Kings 17:1, emphasis added). God honored Elijah's word.

Through the finished work of Jesus, there is a place where you also walk in the Spirit. Even while living with flesh, you can minister from the heavens. You can connect time and eternity. The flesh is not meant to cripple you, but only to keep you touchable to creation. You can bring heaven to the earthly realm and affect physical realities by the Spirit. Praise God in what He is able to accomplish through us!

If you try to force God into the natural, into something tangible—then you limit Him. We often put God into a box, and try to define Him by our own expectations. God is Lord over creation, and can cause the sun to go backwards. He holds time in His very hands. He exists over and above our earthly limitations.

Immanent God

Is God big enough to establish the Law and then fulfill that same Law in Jesus—not because the former was a mistake, but because it was all part of His plan? Yes! God wanted to show us our need for a savior. Our flesh is of a stubborn nature with a stubborn personality. Through the Law, we are able to see just how stubborn it is. It cannot be tamed by a measly offering. In the Old Testament, people needed to constantly offer sacrifices because they fell repeatedly. They were slaves to sin. The Law was the first phase in God's plan for humanity, allowing us to grasp the truth about our fallen natures. The second phase was Jesus—the fullness of God—becoming flesh and dwelling among us.

The Bible says that Jesus came to fulfill the Law (Matthew 5:17). God Himself became a human, limited to soul, spirit, and body. He took on the form that we inherited from our ancestor Adam. After the first phase was completed, God showed us the higher way of approaching Him. He fulfilled the Old Covenant and brought in a New Covenant. He gave life to the new man so that the old man could die. The Lord Jesus showed us that we could walk in righteousness, as He did. He showed us that we could walk in the miraculous, like He did. All the works He displayed, He called His followers to do. He said, "Most assuredly, I say to you, he who believes in Me, the works that I do he will do also; and greater works than these he will do, because I go to My Father" (John 14:12). When we live by the Spirit—the very Spirit of God that raised Jesus from the dead—we walk as Jesus walked.

Jesus became flesh. Flesh serves an important purpose in this realm. It allows us to be touched by the feelings and infirmities of the people. That's what being in the flesh is for; we have to remain a priesthood that is touchable. When the Lord became flesh, he could be touched by the frailties of a fallen creation. God gave us His Spirit and restored us to His very image. As spiritual beings we can operate in the realm of the flesh through His finished work. We are equipped to bring God's goodness to a creation in desperate need of Him. People are hurting. In addition to a spiritual awakening, they also need to be ministered to in their flesh.

We can minister to creation by calling forth light—something we will examine in great detail in the following chapter.

Chapter 8
Let There Be Light

In the beginning God created the heavens and the earth. The earth was without form, and void; and darkness was on the face of the deep. And the Spirit of God was hovering over the face of the waters.

Then God said, "Let there be light"; and there was light. And God saw the light, that it was good; and God divided the light from the darkness. God called the light Day, and the darkness He called Night.

—Genesis 1:1-5

Creating Darkness and Forming Light

Genesis 1 is very familiar passage of Scripture. It is here that we discover the process of creation. I find it interesting that when God was establishing the world, as we know it, He did not ever address the darkness. Instead, He addressed the light, which came out of the darkness. In Isaiah 45:7 God says, "I form the light and create darkness." The Scriptures tell us that darkness was *created*, but light was *formed*. The light was always there, waiting to be formed by God. In contrast, the darkness had to be created. It has a beginning and an end. God called forth the light from the darkness, and He calls us to do the same.

The Church has excelled in creating darkness. We create darkness through our vindictive words. We create darkness by limiting God's power in our understanding. We create darkness by giving the devil credit where no credit is due. We give the devil credit when our own words and works captivate us. When we give him attention, we give him power. When we fight the devil, we are fighting the wrong battle. The real battle is in our own minds. The real battle is not with*out*, but with*in*. When we don't acknowledge this, we lend to the creation of darkness.

We need to be enlightened. We need to realize that the devil is not all-powerful. God is Lord over creation, over *all* of creation. God created the darkness, and thus, has control over it. God gives us peace that passes understanding in the midst of darkness (Philippians 4:7). He does not want us to be preoccupied with darkness. We need to break up our love affair with the devil.

Rather than handle darkness, it's time for you to learn how to handle light. It's time for you to learn how to handle excess, overflow. It's time for you to learn how to handle the miraculous. I'm fully persuaded that we haven't yet received the fullness God has promised us because we haven't learned how to form light. In order to learn how to call the light out of darkness, we have to shift our attention from dark to light.

Anybody can handle darkness in the name of Jesus; but the light is waiting for its command. We are going to learn how to form light, compact it, and bring it together to become substance. Our preoccupation with the devil must end. Why would you wrestle with darkness when you can command the light? It is time for you to come out of darkness and be who God has called you to be.

Two Tests

Jesus had two tests. The first test came before Jesus started his ministry, when He was tempted by the devil. This test was from the outside. Matthew tells us: "Then Jesus was led up by the Spirit into the wilderness to be tempted by the devil" (Matthew 4:1). The devil tempted Jesus, but it was the *Holy Spirit* who led Jesus to the place of temptation. The devil was used as an instrument to test the *motives* of Jesus as a flesh-man; but the Spirit proved Him to be tried and true. The devil gave Him opportunity to compromise, but God used the opportunity to reveal the purity of Jesus' heart and mind.

Galatians 5:24 tells us: "And those who are Christ's have crucified the flesh with its passions and desires." God isn't going to test your flesh, because the flesh has to be crucified. The flesh contains no good thing (Romans 7:18). If you are being tested in the flesh you are set up for failure because your flesh cannot adjust to the Kingdom. God doesn't test the flesh—He crucifies it in Christ, so that a new life may grow. He transforms us by the renewing of the mind (Romans 12:2). We are to put on the mind of Christ. If we concentrate on the flesh, we are hindering the light.

Once you put on the mind of Christ and love God with all your heart, the Holy Spirit may test your motives. He may test your heart and mind. Don't mistake this test for the work of the devil. The devil is only an instrument, used to sharpen you for greater things. James tells us: "Blessed is the man who endures temptation; for when he has been approved, he will receive the crown of life which the Lord has promised to those who love Him" (James 1:12).

The second test of Jesus was the test of His will. This test was from the inside. Right before His crucifixion, Jesus prayed in the Garden of Gethsemane. Luke recorded His earnest prayer:

> "Father, if it is Your will, take this cup away from Me; nevertheless not My will, but Yours, be done." Then an angel appeared to Him from heaven, strengthening Him. And being in agony, He prayed more earnestly. Then His sweat became like great drops of blood falling down to the ground.
>
> —Luke 22:42-44

Jesus had a will, just like any human being. He asked the Father if it was possible for Him to bypass the crucifixion. He was wrestling with two wills—His will and the Father's will. You will only wrestle with two wills in your life, and one of them is not the will of the devil. You will wrestle with God's will and your own will.

God has promised us: "For I know the thoughts that I think toward you, saith the Lord, thoughts of peace, and not of evil, to give you an expected end" (Jeremiah 29:11, KJV). God knows His plan for us. He knows our ultimate destination. The only question remaining is how we want to get there. Do you want to reach that expected end your way or God's way? The second test you will go through is the test of your will. The Church is up against this test right now.

There's a pattern that you go through to move to the place where you can handle light. Your heart, your mind, and your motives have to be tested. Before you can learn to form light, you must pass both the test from the outside as well as the test from the inside.

Receiving Our Full Inheritance

From the foundation of the world, there is an inheritance that has been reserved for us. That inheritance is not limited to the realm of the Church, but is inclusive of the entirety of creation. It encompasses everything that has breath. A portion of that inheritance is the unbeliever. In the Psalms, God says, "Ask of me, and I shall give thee the heathen for thine inheritance, and the uttermost parts of the earth for thy possession" (Psalm 2:8, KJV). The Church has not walked in the fullness of its inheritance, because part of that inheritance includes the unbeliever. Too often, we lack God's passion for the lost and hurting of this world. Like Jonah, we would rather see people get what's coming to them instead of share the Gospel with them.

We must realize that nobody wants to remain in sin. Nobody wants to experience hell. Their eyes are blinded and their minds are deceived. They desperately need the Word of God. Jesus said, "Those who are well have no need of a physician, but those who are sick. I did not come to call the righteous, but sinners, to repentance" (Mark 2:17). We are called to bring forth the light and command the light to shine over darkness. We must come to terms with the fact that we don't get to choose who we give life to. God tells the light to go where it should go. A day will come when we will release life to *all* of creation.

Jesus Christ is the Light that lights every man's life. The Gospel of John declares:

> In the beginning was the Word, and the Word was with God, and the Word was God. He was in the beginning with God. All things were made through Him, and without Him nothing was made that was made. In Him was life, and the life was the light of men. And the light shines in the darkness, and the darkness did not comprehend it.
>
> There was a man sent from God, whose name was John. This man came for a witness, to bear witness of the Light, that all through him might believe. He was not that Light, but was sent to bear witness of that Light. That was

the true Light which gives light to every man coming into the world.

—John 1:1-9

John says that the true Light gives light *to every man coming into the world.* Everybody that comes into the world has the potential of light. You know what's wrong? Nobody is speaking to that light. I'm fully persuaded that God is not playing catch up. God has made provision and God has made a way, if only we find the keys.

God said there is a priesthood that will inherit the heathen. We receive the heathen for our inheritance because of God's love for them. He wants them to be handled tenderly. He handled you tenderly, so why wouldn't you treat the unbeliever in the same way? God wants to give you the heathen. God wants to give you the unbeliever. God wants to give you those dwelling in darkness so that you can speak the light into existence. If He can trust you, God is going to teach you how to form light.

Command the Light

Paul tells us: "For we do not preach ourselves, but Christ Jesus the Lord, and ourselves your bondservants for Jesus' sake. For it is the God who commanded light to shine out of darkness..." (2 Corinthians 4:5-6a).

We have been busy creating darkness, wrestling with darkness, talking about darkness, and rebuking darkness. We are working hard and sweating trying to command the darkness. We're trying to control the darkness. We're trying to rebuke, bind, and loose the darkness. Let's stop wasting our time! There is a *higher* way. Instead of commanding the darkness, let's learn how to command the light.

So how do you command light? How do you form light? How does light come forth from darkness? God called the light from the darkness by commanding it to be. He spoke it into existence. God teaches us to command the light by calling things that are not as though they were (Romans 4:17). In order to form the light, we must learn to call things as God says they are. We must look past the darkness and see with the very eyes of God.

When you come across darkness in your life, command the light to come forth. Every trial that you go through has light hidden inside, waiting to be called out. Let's form the light. Let's find the light. Let's call forth things that are not as though they were. Let's bring into existence the things of God. Our vision will line up with God's when we receive a revelation of Him and His purpose. We will be able to materialize light from darkness after we understand His revelation.

Seek Revelation

Paul tells us in Corinthians:

> But we speak the wisdom of God in a mystery, the hidden wisdom which God ordained before the ages for our glory, which none of the rulers of this age knew; for had they known, they would not have crucified the Lord of glory.

But as it is written:

"Eye has not seen, nor ear heard,
Nor have entered into the heart of man
The things which God has prepared for those
who love Him."

But God has revealed them to us through His
Spirit.

—1 Corinthians 2:7-10a

How do we learn to form light? We learn to form light through revelation. It is not a skill that can be mechanically applied; it has to be revealed to us. The Spirit searches the deep things of God, the mysteries of God. There is a depth in prayer we haven't yet touched because we've been fooling with the darkness instead of forming light. And when you learn to form light, all things will begin to work together.

The first form God wants light to take is faithfulness. Begin to form faithfulness in your life. Be faithful in the little things to show God that you can handle more (Luke 16:10). Be faithful in prayer. Be faithful in dying to yourself and choosing to let God's will override your own. Light is a powerful thing that cannot be treated lightly or handled by everybody. Ask God to teach you how to handle the light in your life. Ask Him what form He wants it to take. Surrender your own will and begin to see with God's vision.

Darkness was created, but the light has always been. The reason why God says "Let there be light" and the light was

(Genesis 1:3), is because light was always there. God called it forth. Darkness, on the other hand, is temporary. The devil knows his time is short. God has set the boundaries. Darkness does not understand the light (John 1:5). When light appears, darkness flees. All the darkness knows is that when we call forth the light, it comes. All it knows is that when we speak light, light dispels the darkness. Light is in control, not darkness.

Let's go into prayer with this knowledge. Go into your life equipped with it. Command the light to be manifested in your life. Ask God to teach you about His glory and His brightness. Ask God to teach you, and you will not be disappointed.

When we receive a revelation from the Lord, what should we do with it? The Bible says that when the Virgin Mary learned of the appearance of angels to the shepherds concerning the birth of Jesus, she "kept all these things and pondered them in her heart" (Luke 2:19). After we receive a revelation, we *contemplate* it and *ponder* it in our hearts. We think about what God wants to accomplish.

Right before God said, "Let there be light," Scripture says He was "hovering over the face of the waters" (Genesis 1:2). Before we form light, we need to hover, contemplate, and ponder. It may help to get some pictures of what your life is supposed to look like, and lay them in front of you. Imagine what it is that God wants to accomplish. Visualize His revelation and His will manifest in your life. As you hover over it, God will teach you how to form it into reality. Get some pictures, write the vision, make your plan, and then do what you see the Father doing (John 5:19).

How do you form light? It takes revelation, thought, and contemplation. God will trust you with more light as you hover, ponder, decree, and declare.

Adjust Your Vision

God said, "Let there be light." He never addressed the darkness, he never spoke to the darkness, he never thought about the darkness. He spoke to the light. We've been feeding darkness, creating darkness. God tells us of a higher way. God teaches us how to command the light. He teaches us to form the light in our lives. He teaches us to bring the light together to manifest what He has revealed to us. Darkness can't stop it!

Our minds are being renewed, because God wants us to go beyond creating darkness. He wants a people that know how to handle light. There is power in light. In the Sermon on the Mount, Jesus says, "The lamp of the body is the eye. If therefore your eye is good, your whole body will be full of light. But if your eye is bad, your whole body will be full of darkness. If therefore the light that is in you is darkness, how great is that darkness!" (Matthew 6:22-23). It's all about how you see. If you see yourself as fighting the devil your whole life and barely winning, then the light that's in your eye is darkness.

We have to adjust our vision. We have to adjust our eyesight so that we see by the Spirit rather than the flesh. The book of Revelation talks about the Church of Laodicea:

> Because you say, "I am rich, have become wealthy, and have need of nothing"—and do not know that you are wretched, miserable, poor, blind, and naked—I counsel you to buy from Me gold refined in the fire, that you may be rich; and white garments, that you may be clothed, that the shame of your nakedness may not be revealed; and anoint your eyes with eye salve, that you may see. As many as I love, I rebuke and chasten. Therefore be zealous and repent.
> —Revelation 3:17-19

We have to allow God to adjust our vision. If God loves you, He will refine you. If you are a son, He will refine you. If you intend to be used by Him and move in the ministry, He will circumcise not only your flesh, but also your heart and your mind. He will deal with your thinking, feelings, and motives. He will deal with the issues of your heart that you've been holding on to for years.

We must quit talking to darkness and ask God to teach us how to form light. When you know how to from light, you know how to bring heaven to earth. The kingdoms of this world shall become the Kingdoms of our Lord and of His Christ, and He shall reign forever (Revelation 11:15). God is not going to abandon the earth. The earth and everything in it belongs to the Lord (Psalm 24:1). God needs a priesthood to stand between Him and the world to make intercession—and that priesthood will be Melchizedek. Melchizedek ministers after the endless source of life and light. Melchizedek knows how to handle light. That's where you are called.

We are going into a new place. God wants our hearts, minds, and wills. He wants us to seek His revelation and ponder it. He wants our vision adjusted. He wants us to command the light. God wants us to move in a higher realm—a realm of mastery.

Chapter 9
A Realm Called Mastery

True mastery is the manifestation of the fullness of son-ship expressed in a people *walking as* God, rather than simply *walking with* God. It is embracing God's agenda over our own. Holiness is necessary in order to walk in mastery, and can only be realized when we live in a realm where all motivation comes from a pure heart that is expressed from within and overflows to the outside.

The Meaning of Holiness

Precious brothers and sisters, let us be holy. Over the years many people have given weight to external matters in an effort to define holiness. This should not be so. It is helpful to dismiss these mistaken notions in order to understand the truth about holiness. Let us see with the vision of God rather than judge with the human eye.

1. Holiness has nothing to do with outer appearance.

Throughout the Gospels Jesus warns against the hypocrisy of the scribes and Pharisees, who loved to wear the appearance of godliness, but did not know God at all in their hearts. He says, "Beware of the scribes, who desire to go around in long robes, love greetings in the marketplaces, the best seats in the synagogues, and the best places at feasts, who devour widows' houses, and for a pretense make long prayers. These will receive greater condemnation" (Luke 20:46). He teaches people that true holiness isn't what others see on the outside, but rather what God sees on the inside.

Jesus reveals the futility of focusing on outward appearance without having the right heart on the inside. He challenges the authorities in Jerusalem: "Woe to you, scribes and Pharisees, hypocrites! For you cleanse the outside of the cup and dish, but inside they are full of extortion and self-indulgence. Blind Pharisee, first cleanse the inside of the cup and dish, that the outside of them may be clean also" (Matthew 23:25-26). Holiness does not come from the outside, but rather from the inside; "Not what goes into the mouth defiles a man; but what comes out of the mouth, this defiles a man" (Matthew 15:11).

I remember when women were expected to keep their head covered in church. One time the church ran out of doilies. In keeping with their tradition, they had to pin toilet paper on my head instead. It might sound funny and ridiculous in retrospect—but at the time it was a very serious matter.

Creation needs revelation. They do not need the doctrines and opinions of man. They do not need toilet paper as makeshift coverings on their heads. Creation needs life through the new man, led by the Holy Spirit. Melchizedek is that life. Holiness describes that way of life. It is a realm, a way of thinking, a way of acting, and a way of fellowship. Holiness is a way of seeing, not with a natural eye, but seeing as God sees.

2. **Holiness is not about what we do, as if we could earn God's favor.**

Jesus said there were a people that worshipped Him with their mouths, but their hearts were far from Him (Matthew 15:8). Jesus also said:

> Many will say to Me in that day, "Lord, Lord, have we not prophesied in Your name, cast out demons in Your name, and done many wonders in Your name?" And then I will declare to them, "I never knew you; depart from Me, you who practice lawlessness!"
> —Matthew 7:22-23

Jesus says He never *knew* those people. That word *knew* is also used in Jeremiah when God said, "Before I formed you in the womb I *knew* you..." (Jeremiah 1:5a, emphasis added). It goes back to Genesis when Adam *knew* Eve (Genesis 4:1). Jesus is effectively saying to the people, "You used my name, but there was never any intimacy there." There are people who act religious, who understand the religious language, and who even use the name of the Lord—but they have yet to let God work inside of them. They haven't submitted to His lordship.

There is only one thing that can hinder the Word of the God. Jesus told the people that their traditions made the Word of God of no effect (Mark 7:13a). The only thing that can hinder the Word is tradition, religion, and man's doctrine. The devil can't stop the Word of God; your own bad attitude cannot hinder what God wants to accomplish. Nothing is strong enough to hinder the Word except the tradition and religion of man.

We reduce Christianity to a "religion of man" when we make it about our external actions. Holiness is not found in our actions, but is rather an attitude of the heart. Praying, fasting, and being still before the Lord are necessary; in fact, Scripture prescribes them. But in and of themselves, they do not equal holiness. "For by grace you have been saved through faith, and that not of yourselves; it is the gift of God, not of works, lest anyone should boast (Ephesians 2:8-9). It is not about our own works.

126

Holiness is an attitude. "To the pure, all things are pure..." (Titus 1:15). It is a heart that sees its deficiency without God, and longs for a complete manifestation of Him. You may not be perfect now, but trying to do the best you can counts for something. God sees your will and intent, and honors that. We grow day by day as we walk this journey out. He causes us to grow and mature. God will bring wholeness to your life. It comes little by little, line upon line, precept upon precept. God is a progressive and ever-expanding God.

3. **Holiness is letting go of guilt and shame—which will cripple you.**

I used to feel so guilty all the time that I was constantly apologizing. One time I apologized to my brother and he responded, "You already apologized about that last year. And you also apologized for something that happened when we were six, and I have no idea what you are talking about."

You might slip up or say something nasty, but repent and move on. God is not more pleased with you when you cripple yourself searching for undiscovered sin. Being overly introspective may seem "holy" but in reality it's actually very selfish, and exposes a lack of trust in your heart. Nobody can convict like the Holy Spirit can (John 16:8). Be sensitive to Him, and then leave him to do His job. Trust Him to not leave you in the dark. It's not your job to be constantly obsessed with your mistakes and failures; it's your job to heed the voice of God. When He convicts you, make amends and move on. Grace and mercy are beautiful things.

The apostle Paul writes: "For I know that in me (that is, in my flesh) nothing good dwells; for to will is present with me, but how to perform what is good I do not find. For the good that I will to do, I do not do; but the evil I will not to do, that I practice" (Romans 7:18-19).

The apostle Paul—who was caught up to the third heaven, and heard things that man could not utter—said this. This is the same Paul who wrote two thirds of the New Testament; who had such an overflow of the Spirit in his life that it spilled over onto his apron. That apron was then cut up and passed among the people to receive healing (Acts 19:11-12). The anointing saturated not only his body, but the very clothes he wore. This same apostle says that there is a war going on in his members (Romans 7:23). If he had issues, then you will probably have to deal with some issues as well.

Now, don't misunderstand what I am saying—I am not trying to say that sin is okay. I am saying that our own growth will be hindered if we sit around repenting all day. God is not pleased when you dwell on your mistakes—in fact He paid a high price to *remove* that sin from you—and we think it's "holy" to cling to it? Through Christ we're given a new identity! Let's praise God for that and walk in that new identity, instead of choosing to live in condemnation under the old man.

Your flesh is never going to cooperate with God. Your mind won't either. Both must be brought under subjection to the Spirit of God. Maturity does not happen overnight. Growth is progressive. After you have repented, move on.

It is not a holy practice for you to be hard on yourself. God loves you. Love keeps no record of wrong (1 Corinthians 13:4-7). God is not recording your failures. On the road to fullness, God can be trusted to deal with the issues in you that need to be dealt with. He gives us the grace to bear correction, come to a higher way of thinking, and continue in growth. He is bringing us to a place, but it is progressive. Do not be disappointed when you are not perfect overnight.

4. **Holiness perseveres through struggles.**

Why do Christians often feel that being born again means that they should be exempt from experiencing the normal difficulties and struggles of life? The Scripture says it rains on the just and unjust alike (Matthew 5:45). Everyone experiences hard times. Things are going to happen in your life to enable you to grow, things that you will be required to overcome and to move past. Things will happen to elevate your way of thinking, to elevate your language, to elevate your behavior, and to move you to a higher place of maturity in God. Never having challenges, never having to deal with mistakes—it sounds wonderful, but no growth takes place. You would never mature!

Jesus says, "I am the true vine, and My Father is the vinedresser. Every branch in Me that does not bear fruit He takes away; and every branch that bears fruit He prunes, that it may bear more fruit" (John 15:1-2). In order for you to grow and mature, there must be seasons of purging in your life.

Could it be that God is already seeing some fruit in your life, and He knows that if He prunes you and cuts away excess baggage—more fruit will be produced? Greater understanding and the multiplication of fruit in your heart and mind come with pruning. Cutting things off that are still attached will not feel good. It won't be an enjoyable process. But your Heavenly Father knows His plan for you, and what will be best for you in the end. Trust Him with your life, even through difficulties. Purging is that test on the inside, and you must pass that test before promotion.

Everything in your life is not going to be peaches and cream. There are some things in your life that may not always be wonderful. We are growing from faith to faith, glory to glory, and realm to realm. You are being conformed into the image of Jesus. You are the clay and He is the potter. God told Jeremiah to come down to the pottery house to see how clay is molded in the hands of the Potter (Jeremiah 18:2-4). Remain malleable in His hands!

5. **Holiness is embodied in confident living—not desperation, hopelessness, or fear.**

Many times people pray as trials come, asking God to remove the trials from their lives. If a problem arises, they come before God in prayer with fears, worries, and insecurities. Uncomfortable situations tend to distract people. People get distracted when it looks like they won't get their own way, or when their motives are questioned.

As Christians face purging, the essential issue isn't to avoid or escape the process. Instead, you should manifest Christ at *all times*. We must face life as a visible expression of an invisible God.

There is a way to face life where the end-goal is simply to survive and remain in one piece; and there is a way to face life where we manifest Christ and experience growth and maturity, pointing other people to God along the way. The choice is yours. Life happens. The experiences of life are designed to assist us in remaining touchable to creation, resulting in growth and maturity.

6. **Holiness is letting God do His business on His terms.**

God can purge any person, place, or thing from your life. If it looks like someone is not headed down the same path you are, it may be because they don't *want* to go there. Don't try to force them. We are not burdened with the task of producing fruit in others. Many Christians are content with the guarantee of heaven, and aren't necessarily seeking the fullness that God has to offer. It is only natural and good to desire for our loved ones to seek God in His fullness— but we can't *make* that happen.

We should plant seeds, and then stand back to let the Holy Spirit bring growth. If we are not careful we may spend too much time checking on the seed, and trample the soil in the process. We can actually hinder the work of God by trying too hard. Trust God to bring the full harvest. Leave things alone.

God purges people, things, thoughts, ideas, and agendas. He purges them from your life so that you can move on. Be at peace with this. You cannot make people repent; I have tried and can testify that it doesn't work. Let it go.

So we understand that holiness is not derived from outer appearance, external actions, guilt, hopelessness, a trial-free life, or taking control of other people's lives. Rather holiness is a mode of thinking, a state of mind, and a condition of the heart. Holiness flows from the inward self to the outward, supernaturally affecting our actions, thoughts, emotions, and motives. Above all, holiness is laying down your own agenda to walk as God.

The Anointing

God uses the anointing to quicken mortal flesh. It breaks every yolk—everything hindering us from walking in the realm of mastery. The anointing allows God to increase in us. It is not something that you can fast, pray, and work your way into. The anointing does not come through sweat. Flesh and blood does not inherit the Kingdom of God. It is not by works lest any man should boast (Ephesians 2:8-9). At the end of the day, God calls us to be transformed by the renewing of the mind. There is absolutely nothing you can do to become godly in your flesh. You have to be born again, not of corruptible seed but of incorruptible seed, which is the Word of God.

The anointing is free, but it is not cheap. It was bought with the costly blood of Jesus. You cannot pay for it, nor can you suffer for it—yet it will cost you everything. In order to receive the anointing, you will have to give up your own ideas, agendas, and motives—and even take every thought captive for Christ (2 Corinthians 10:5). Most people are eager to receive it—until they realize that they must give up their own egos. It is no longer about *you* or what *you* want. The anointing requires that we submit all things to God, and deny ourselves (Luke 9:23).

Under the Old Covenant, the priests entering the inner court were not to "clothe themselves with anything that causes sweat" (Ezekiel 44:18). We are not called to sweat. The anointing comes freely with God's favor. This does not, however, mean that we won't experience suffering. When you suffer, it won't be for the anointing. Suffering will be used for maturity and growth.

The spiritual disciplines don't give access to the anointing, but they prepare you to be a good steward of the anointing. For instance, you can fast to bring your flesh into subjection, so that you can concentrate or become single-minded. Jesus was the Word made flesh; we are flesh being made the Word. Preparation and stewardship are necessary because the anointing is a powerful thing. The Church is called to be prepared; not on the outside but on the inside.

A part of your internal preparation involves studying the Scriptures and allowing them to work personally within you. I believe that anybody who wants the anointing of God to rest within them in any measure must have a full working knowledge of the Scriptures. There is no substitution for knowing the Scripture. The Scripture is God's personality. The Scripture is the expression of the way God thinks. When you become familiar with how God works and thinks, you may not always need a "word" from other people. When the Word of God takes root in your heart, that inward witness will wax stronger and stronger. Remember, God's ways may not always seem better, but they are always higher than our ways.

The Supernatural Realm

The supernatural enables us to move beyond the flesh. It is a place beyond human reasoning or understanding. It is a place of timelessness. Unfortunately, the supernatural still scares many people in the Church. What they neglect to understand is that the Kingdom itself operates within the supernatural!

Fear hath torment (1 John 4:18). Fear about how God works causes us to create doctrines that box Him in. Having the security of a doctrine created by man feels better than living with an unanswered question. Having a God that always acts a certain way is preferable over a God that can act unpredictably and supernaturally. We are often afraid to let Him work in His own way. The Pharisees certainly had an exhaustive picture of how God was supposed to act, based on the Old Testament. Their pre-conceived notions blinded them from recognizing God Himself, walking amongst them. In fact, Jesus was so contrary to their expectations that they had Him crucified!

Fear will cause you to obsess over all the wrong questions. When is God going to do this? How is God going to do it? If He did it like that before, then why wouldn't He do it like that again? If God could really heal, then why did my friend die of that disease? In our own feeble attempts to answer our unanswered questions, we draw false conclusions. We believe that God can only act in a certain way. We believe that any evidence that conflicts with our viewpoint or opinion is misguided and wrong. Having a Pharisaical or religious outlook on God blinds us from the reality of who He is. Even if a miracle were performed right in front of our eyes, we'd have the ability to explain it away! Let's allow God to be God, however He wants to be God.

Sometimes our fear causes us to create a plan B. When God told Abraham that he and Sarah would have a son, he didn't take God at His word. He thought about all the possible ways that this could come to pass in a more believable way, instead of having a simple, child-like faith in the power of God. He had one born in his house, Eliazar, just in case God did not give him a son (Genesis 15:2-3). Abraham was afraid of God's promise not coming to pass. He was afraid that God would not do it in a timely manner. He was concerned by *how* God was going to do it.

Sarah also had a plan B. She said to Abraham, "See now, the Lord has restrained me from bearing children. Please, go in to my maid; perhaps I shall obtain children by her" (Genesis 16:2). She didn't think that God could fulfill His promise using her own womb; so she devised her own plan, to fulfill the word of God in her own terms. She didn't have faith to take God at His word.

God did not buy into their plans. He waited until Abraham was "as good as dead" (Hebrews 11:12; Romans 4:19). He wanted the promise to manifest through the supernatural— not through Abraham's or Sarah's efforts and ideas.

At the end of the day, Abraham and Sarah were afraid because they were trying to save face. They wanted to protect God's reputation, as well as their own. What would

Abraham tell the people if God did not do what He said He was going to do? How would people perceive him as a man chasing after the word of an incompetent God? He was planning on making an excuse on God's behalf. He would have said, "It's okay, God kept His promise! I've had one born in my house that I have raised—that's who God was talking about."

The problem is that God never asks us to make excuses for Him! He only asks us to trust Him. Trying to protect God's reputation is suggestive of fear and torment. Trying to protect our own reputations reveals a lack of faith, and a desire to please men above God. God does not need for us to worry about His reputation, and He never asks us to work to please men. God is not like man, and He does not conform to the opinions of man. God will prove Himself, all by Himself.

When we come to a place of fearlessness, we come to a place of trust. We are no longer tormented by the details. We no longer try to figure God out. There is no "Plan B".

When we get to the place where we are not afraid, we move in a place of timelessness in God. There is no pressure because we understand that God does what He wants to do, how He wants to do it, in His own time frame. We have the opportunity to become willing participants with Him and take part in what He is already accomplishing. He is already on the move. He is already God. Let's cooperate and flow in God. He does not need our help.

Reaping Comes After Sowing

Luke 6:38 says, "Give, and it shall be given unto you; good measure, pressed down, and shaken together, and running over, shall men give into your bosom. For with the same measure that ye mete withal it shall be measured to you again" (King James Version).

All that is pressed down, shaken together, and running over comes from man. Imagine what happens when God steps in. What kind of reaping will you then be permitted to do? In Malachi, God says:

> "Bring all the tithes into the storehouse,
> That there may be food in My house,
> And try Me now in this,"
> Says the Lord of hosts,
> "If I will not open for you the windows of heaven
> And pour out for you such blessing
> That there will not be room enough to receive it"
> —Malachi 3:10

When God steps in, He will give beyond what you have asked or imagined! (Ephesians 3:20).

We have given our time, our tithes, our seed, and our offering. The Lord tells us that when we give, it will be given back to us, overflowing. We shall receive it back pressed down, shaken together, and running over. God is going to make room in you. He is going to expand you. He is going to press you, shake you, and stretch you until you can contain overflow. It might not be comfortable to be pressed down and shaken, but God must stretch you for real overflow. He does not want to leave any room in you, or any empty spaces. He wants to bless you through and through. But we cannot experience the fullness of God's blessing without the giving up of ourselves. When we give, we make room for the overflow of God. We must be willing to sow in order to reap the harvest.

God has invited us to eat of His goodness:

> Oh, taste and see that the Lord is good;
> Blessed is the man who trusts in Him!
> —Psalm 34:8

God is calling us to a place of mastery where we have more than enough. When we hoard blessings by keeping them to ourselves, we stop the flow. When we don't trust God enough to sow, we set ourselves up to experience the hardship that we've created in our own minds. We hinder God from working. When we are faithful with our blessings, we understand that the blessings come to us, but they are not all ours to keep. God often uses us to be distributers of His wealth and blessing. When we share the blessing of God, we experience more increase and overflow. God can see that we have been faithful, and He will continue to pour into us.

Our attitudes toward giving, sowing, and sharing will determine the reality of our own lives. When we give freely as an extension of our very natures through Christ, realizing that God gives freely to us, we experience no lack. We understand who God is calling us to be. When fear is our motivation for storing up for ourselves, we operate according to the wisdom of the world. We live beneath God's standard for our lives. The kind of harvest we reap depends on how accurately we hear from God. It is important to sow according to wisdom and instruction, and not merely emotion. We must hear from God. We don't scatter seed; we prayerfully sow seed into good ground.

You Have a Purpose

You are being prepared for something. You are not here by accident; He chose you in Him from before the foundation of the world. If you did not have a call or a mission to fulfill, He would not have released you to the earth; you would never have been born. You are here because you have an appointment with destiny. Be careful not to think that your parents, as a result of planning or even a mistake, are responsible for your presence in the earth. God wants to use you to accomplish something in this generation that only you can do!

The minute you consecrate yourself to God and ask for His guidance, He will not turn you away. If you ask God to make His purpose for your life known, He will not leave you wondering. You may not see the whole picture all at once; He may only reveal the first portion of the path while the rest remains obscure. You don't have to know every detail all the time. But as you trust in Him to continue to guide you little by little, step by step, you will not be disappointed. God wants you to fulfill your destiny, but that can only be done through faith.

The Scriptures tell us to love God, serve him, and seek His Kingdom first; and then everything else will be added to us (Matthew 6:33). All of these things are added. They are coming to you. You will begin to see blessings in your life. You will discover avenues of blessings you never considered. When you come into your right mind, you begin to see clearly. When you lift your eyes up, there is a field ready for harvest that you did not work for. Lift your eyes up and you will see that the harvest is already here. Open your understanding. Prepare for mastery.

Epilogue

A More Excellent Way

God has gifted each of us individually. We each excel and serve God in different ways in order to build up His creation. There are apostles, teachers, miracles workers, healers, and those gifted in speaking and interpreting tongues (1 Corinthians 12:27-31). Yet Paul tells us in Corinthians that without love, all of the gifts are meaningless! (1 Corinthians 13). The greatest gift—and the most excellent way—is love. The mark of God's true sons is that they will walk in love (John 13:35). Everything flows from that realm of love.

The Old Testament says that the prophet Daniel had an "excellent spirit" and distinguished himself above many in Darius' kingdom (Daniel 6:3). His enemies plotted against him but could find no fault in him (Daniel 6:4). Daniel moved so high that his spirit is often sought to be duplicated today. His way was excellent. And yet, the New Testament revelation of love is *better* than excellent. It is a *more* excellent way.

The Scripture tells us: "Beloved, let us love one another, for love is of God; and everyone who loves is born of God and knows God. He who does not love does not know God, for God is love" (1 John 4:7-8). God actually embodies love. Love is that part of God that cannot fail. The only thing in creation that does not fail, is love. Paul imparts this truth: "Love never fails. But whether there are prophecies, they will fail; whether there are tongues, they will cease; whether there is knowledge, it will vanish away" (1 Corinthians 13:8). Love can never fail. All of creation is subject to a finish or failure. Tongues cease, knowledge passes away. We know in part and prophesy in part, but "God Love" never fails.

Love is a mystery. We see through a glass darkly, but when love is perfected or allowed to mature, everything else falls away and we see clearly with both eyes. Perfected love casts out even fear (1 John 4:18). There is no room for anything else to coexist with love in its purest and most undefiled form. Love contains the fullness of God; anything other than His perfect love is tainted with our own egos. It is of a lower realm, mixed with self, opinions, ideas, and personal agendas. It is a product of our own performance. Perfected love is all God, and only God.

There are only two masters in this life, and one of those is not the devil (Matt 6:24). There is God and mammon—and you will serve one! There are only two kinds of love—God Love or love of money. The Bible tells us that the love of money is the root of all evil (1 Timothy 6:10). On the contrary, God Love is the foundation for all Truth. God Love is the most excellent way. It propels us into the realm of mastery. It helps us to see with the eyes of God. It empowers us to put away the flesh and walk in the Spirit. You decide what kind of love you walk in.

The Unity of Love

Perfected love brings all things together in unity. It is evidence of our oneness with God: "No one has seen God at any time. If we love one another, God abides in us, and His love has been perfected in us" (1 John 4:12). The Bible tells us that we live, move, and have our being in God (Acts 17:28). Since God is love, then we live, move, and have our being in love. We are nothing outside of it, and accomplish nothing without it. You don't get to choose it; God Love chooses you. It is not something we walk in when we "feel" like it. It is solid and unwavering through every circumstance, seeking to touch every person we come across (Luke 6:35).

Unity with God in perfect love causes us to honor and respect all men, though we may disagree (1 Peter 2:17). Love is matured and perfected when we choose to love one another without judgement. We won't agree with everyone we come across. We don't have to like the life choices that other people make. We don't have to have the exact same doctrines or beliefs as other people—but there will be a respect and honor toward all of creation that exists when we love according to God's standard. The language, clothes, beliefs, and differences in other people are completely irrelevant to love. These things do not mix with love. God Love sees past all outer appearances and actions, and cuts to the heart.

Experience has shown me that if I make other people's business and shortcomings my own, God will not mix Himself with that. He consistently reminds me to deal with my own shortcomings and not those of others. Our responsibility is to see with a love that doesn't judge or condemn in spite of our own personal conviction. This is how we honor and love all men. The Church likes to fuss and fight and disagree. We get it twisted and act like God only loves Christians. By our own petty judgments, we bar others from fellowship. Sometimes the Church—the very people entrusted to reach creation— poses the biggest threat to it. It's time we grow out of those things and enter into the unity of love.

God Love overflows. The very nature of love is that it is meant to be shared with others. It overflows to all of creation. We overflow when we see with the eyes of God. God Love will cut away our flesh until the only thing remaining is Him. Love circumcises the flesh so that we see in the Spirit, and have compassion for other people.

For far too long many have sought to send the unbeliever to an eternal hell, and watch them suffer for eternity. We want them to reap the evil that they have sown. Unfortunately, "burn in hell" has become a very common term. We say it trivially, humorously. This type of perspective will prevent you from inheriting the unbeliever. If only we understood God's burning passion and His undying love for each and every person! It remains the will of the Father to give us the *whole kingdom* (Psalm 2:8). It is not His will that any should perish (2 Peter 3:9). One of the definitions for perish is to render useless. God is intent on using *all* of creation (Psalm 24:1). His true treasure is a *people*. God might have trusted you with money, but can you be trusted with a people? God's alabaster box is His creation. He paid for it with the cross, His life, His blood. Can you be trusted with the alabaster box that He paid for? Does God's passionate love overflow in your soul? Let it be so!

Jesus once told a story to the Jews (Luke 10:30-36). In it, a man was beaten, robbed, and left half dead on the roadside. A priest saw the man lying on the ground, and passed him by. Then a Levite came through, and did the same. But the third man stopped to help. He bandaged the man's wounds, brought him to an inn, and paid his bill. The third man was a Samaritan—a people who were despised by the Jews. A man despised and unloved by those around him took responsibility for the hurts and wounds of a stranger on the roadside. Jesus taught that we should love our neighbors as ourselves, and told this story to illustrate that anybody who is hurt or wounded qualifies as a neighbor. The story of the Good Samaritan demonstrates unconditional love. The religious system (the priest, the law, and the Levites) has passed by wounded creation, but a common man will take responsibily for their wounds without reservation or judgement.

God is preparing a priesthood to come forth that will take responsibility for the lost, the hurting, and the helpless. Love will burst forth from this people unconditionally, with no expectation of receiving anything in return (Matthew 5:46).

The Power of Love

Love is the most powerful force in the universe. In fact, God's entire law is fulfilled by love. All the sacrifices of bulls and goats could not fulfill the law; but love fulfills everything. The Gospel of Mark records a conversation between Jesus and a scribe:

> So the scribe said to Him, "Well said, Teacher. You have spoken the truth, for there is one God, and there is no other but He. And to love Him with all the heart, with all the understanding, with all the soul, and with all the strength, and to love one's neighbor as oneself, is *more* than all the whole burnt offerings and sacrifices."
> —Mark 12:32-33 (emphasis added)

In the Old Testament, the people constantly offered sacrifices to atone for their sin. The power and influence of sin was such that they had to shed blood continually in order to stay right with God. But God's ways are greater than man's. In one single offering of love, God shattered the power of sin forever: "For by one offering He has perfected forever those who are being sanctified" (Hebrews 10:14). God Love is so powerful, it covers a multitude sin (James 5:20; 1 Peter 4:8). It showers mistakes with mercy. Perfected love fulfills all righteousness.

The entire law is fulfilled in love; therefore, trying to interpret it outside of love proves fruitless. The Pharisees once tried to trick Jesus, asking Him what the greatest commandment was. Instead of being puzzled like they were hoping, Jesus answered immediately and decisively:

> Jesus said to him, "'You shall love the Lord your God with all your heart, with all your soul, and with all your mind.' This is the first and great commandment. And the second is like it: 'You shall love your neighbor as yourself.' On these two commandments hang all the Law and the Prophets."
>
> —Matthew 22:37-40

God Love is powerful because it doesn't work from the outside, it works from the inside. Love circumcises the heart and the mind. There is a big difference between God Love and human love. A priesthood that moves in God Love receives the heathen as an inheritance (Ps 2:8). Those walking in love ask for the unbeliever and cry out for those who are lost.

The priesthood that God is calling forth will walk in love. These true sons of God will walk in unity with others. They will walk in the utter power of divine love. They will walk as conquerors in the love of Jesus:

> Yet in all these things we are more than conquerors through Him who loved us. For I am persuaded that neither death nor life, nor angels nor principalities nor powers, nor things present nor things to come, nor height nor depth, nor any other created thing, shall be able to separate us from the love of God which is in Christ Jesus our Lord.
>
> —Romans 8:37-39

God Love is a real love that we have not touched or seen. It is the source of the Melchizedek Priesthood. It is perfected as we put away the flesh and learn to walk in the Spirit. It is the nature of the new man. It fulfills all righteousness and enables us to walk in mastery. The Lord tells us: "But above all these things put on love, which is the bond of perfection" (Col 3:14).

Let love rule. Let love perfect. Put love on and wear it!

My Personal Practice
Whenever we enter a new year, I typically ask God some personal questions as I prepare to experience what He has prepared ahead of me. I will disclose a few of the questions I have contemplated for your consideration: God, how do I grow this year? How do I please you? What should I work on within myself? How do I decrease so that you will increase?

I was shocked to hear God challenge me with these three assignments. He said:

Be delivered from yourself.
Be delivered from people.
And mind your own business.
SELAH!

A Final Word

I hear the Word of the Lord say:

Rejoice, for your mind has been renewed. Overflow is coming and you now know what to do with it. Your thinking has been adjusted. You have been awakened by revelation and you have received. That which used to be last to you, has now become first; and that which used to be first has for you become last. There is a great shift! You have arrived at a realm where you rule and reign. You are no longer just living, no longer just surviving. God has moved you into a fresh understanding. Now there will be a manifestation.

There are only two tests in life: the test of failure and the test of success. You have passed the test of failure. You have given when you had nothing to give. Now, you are being given the test of success, the test of dominion, and the test of overflow. You will pass this test! Put away childish thinking and welcome to your new world.

The Spirit of the Lord sits right in the middle of you. God Himself is ruling and reigning within you. He never desired to be on a physical throne. He desires for *you* to be His throne. His desire is to be seated within a people.

Rejoice. This is your new day.

About the Author

Dr. Connie Williams is a celebrated international teacher, motivational speaker, and life and business coach. For over 35 years she has embraced mankind with a mothering nature while teaching her distinct audiences with an unmistakable, dramatic flair. Throughout childhood, her mother taught her the value of living without judgment, prejudice, or hatred, and to always operate in unconditional love. The fruits of Dr. Connie's upbringing are evident in God's grace upon her to preach His unadulterated Word and allow those from all walks of life to experience His love in a new light: from atheists to life-long believers.

Armed with a strong prophetic gifting, Dr. Connie has prophesied to a diverse range of leaders including those from political, sports, and business industries. Additionally, she has served as a prophetic consultant for both Fortune 500 companies and various entertainment industry projects. She is also a circuit speaker for national and international network programs and conferences, including her own conferences, schools, and leadership institutes.

With authenticity and clarity, Dr. Connie defines herself as a "midwife prophet": one who assists in spiritual delivery, revelation, and proper identification of what God deposits within His people to reach the new realms and dimensions He has ordained.

For more information about

Dr. Connie Williams and Connie Williams International

visit

www.DrConnieWilliams.org

Made in the USA
Middletown, DE
14 May 2017